Praise

'*Customer Improvement Selling* is a must-read for any organisation seeking to optimise its go-to-market approach. By emphasising the often-overlooked role of technical sales and the importance of a cohesive GTM team, this book provides valuable insights backed by research. It highlights the need for effective alignment of commercial approaches between different teams and the significance of providing commercial training to technical teams. A compelling read for anyone invested in sales excellence and organisational success.'

— **Jaren Krchnavi, Head of Sales Enablement**, Siemens Smart Infrastructure, Sales Enablement Collective Ambassador and 2024 Revenue Enablement Excellence Award winner

'Many of today's buyers get stuck when evaluating features and outcomes of highly technical products, a problem that persists in this age of AI. Sellers increasingly involve technical subject matter experts to help convey value and explain how products can achieve the buyers' unique and detailed requirements. Only, too few of these technical experts understand how to meet the moment and act as the technical sellers they need to be. This book provides a roadmap for organizations that want to make their technical experts more effective at impacting client growth and retention.'

— **Ted McKenna**, Bestselling co-author of *The JOLT Effect and The Activator Advantage*

'*Customer Improvement Selling* guides technical experts through the sales process, helping them shape their ideas to help sales teams better meet customer needs. The research in this book demonstrates that most technical experts gain professional satisfaction from contributing to commercial success, but their expertise is not being fully optimized. Anyone interested in gaining more commercial impact will gain new insights into how to get started.'

— **Jennifer McCollum**, CEO and President, Catalyst, Inc.

'*Customer Improvement Selling* is the culmination of the author's two decades worth of experience in building individual, team and organisational capability, while combining tried and tested commercial models with a unique perspective focused on harnessing the power of technical sales. Katarina is an expert at building sales capability across organisations and customer improvement is at the heart of everything she does.'

— **Andrew Marshall**, Strategic Talent Consultant and Australian Human Resources Institute (AHRI) State Council Vice President

'Each department of a business must recognize that they have a role in selling. Technical people who are involved in presales or delivery often have great access to our customers and enjoy high levels of credibility and trust. They have a huge opportunity to identify a buying opportunity and provide invaluable sales leads. So how do we best engage them in the buying journey and how we enable them to get the maximum out of their capabilities? Katarina Coppé, builds on her vast experience in sales enablement and a deep dive into sales studies, by coming up with creative and applicable insights that help technical experts to understand their role in a successful sale. Her book is crisp, solid, insightful and research based. Totally recommended: no sales, no business!'

   — **George Pastidis**, Sales Learning and
      Development Director, Ericsson

'The author masterfully captures both the challenges and opportunities involved in enhancing commercial skills for technical experts. This book is packed with valuable insights and actionable strategies, making it an essential guide for those looking to boost their commercial impact. Beyond being a practical resource for technical professionals, it also serves as a timely reminder for all commercial leaders about the evolving skills required to thrive in today's complex sales environment.'

   — **Maya Garza Ph.D.**, Vice President, Talent and
      Leadership Consulting, TSP, a Syneos Health
      Company

'This is a must-read book for non-salespeople who want to transform themselves from specialists into trusted advisors who can drive growth by solving customer challenges. The COSMOS framework provides a roadmap to make the transition a success and can be applied at both the individual and organisational level. It is clear, easy to follow and immediately applicable for self-driven technical experts and the HR-specialists looking to support them.'

— **Anne Selis**, HR Partner Lead, Accenture Benelux and France

'The author's insights into customer improvement selling finally solve for the perennial challenge in selling -- the best way to bring technical experts and salespeople together to close deals! In an era of increasingly technical solutions, this is essential reading for all business leaders selling IP-driven solutions to customers.'

— **Jean Martin**, Senior Partner, Global Head of Product, Mercer, Marsh Mclennan

'This is a thoughtful and practical approach to fostering a commercial capability across an organisation well beyond the traditional sales team focus. I highly recommend this guide for engaging your technical team in growth for your organisation.'

— **Stephanie Christopher**, Managing Director, Vistage Australia and New Zealand

CUSTOMER IMPROVEMENT SELLING

Unlocking commercial potential in technical experts

Katarina Coppé

R^ethink

First published in Great Britain in 2025
by Rethink Press (www.rethinkpress.com)

Cover image © Shutterstock | afry_harvy

Contents

Introduction

S ales skills and technical expertise are the yin and yang of commercial success: they are capable of doing well apart, but they truly shine when they are put together. Many of the best sales deals I have witnessed or participated in during my twenty-four-year career involved intense cooperation between salespeople and technical experts. This cooperation is probably one of the most important predictors of success for the seller and satisfaction for the customer.

We have entered an era of constant change, interwoven with rapid advances in technology, so business and technical solutions are bound to become more complex, while customers will become more critical about which of those solutions can help to solve their specific challenges. Some salespeople may have enough technical expertise to do well under these conditions, but in most situations it seems wise to invite additional technical expertise into the sales process.

I have always been fascinated by what makes some technical experts drive commercial outcomes so seamlessly even though they are not officially accountable for customer growth, while others would rather stay away from customer interaction or commercial processes.

In the Future of Jobs Report 2023, LinkedIn conducted research into 'Jobs on the Rise' – the 100 fastest and consistently growing roles globally in the last four years.[1] The fastest-growing jobs support sales growth and customer engagement.

In a global talent shortage study, sales and marketing are ranked as the third most important technical skills on a list of the top five 'in demand technical skills', right after IT and data, and engineering.[2] This is not a new trend. A Mercer study in 2018 that included over 7,648 voices across twenty-one industries and forty-four markets predicted that one in three organisations would focus on building sales skills to address the requirements of the future of work.[3]

If organisations cannot find talent with commercial skills, where should we look to solve this critical shortage? Should we attract and select people in a different way? Of course, there are creative ways to recruit sales talent in non-obvious talent pools, and maybe moving away from outdated HR approaches in recruitment or development is now, more than ever before, critical for success in businesses. Some global companies, such as Siemens, encourage their employees to take their career development into their own hands. A person with a technical engineering profile could, for example, aim for a sales role and not only find out their skill gaps, but also receive relevant learning and training recommendations to reach their career goal.

The focus of this book

This book is designed to share what I have learned over the years from working in different disciplines of a business and from the research I have conducted. It covers the foundational findings from different sales and HR research and learnings, based on my own application of them across organisations and countries. Although I will briefly tackle issues in recruitment, which continue to be a barrier to attracting commercial talent, the focus of this book will be more on offering insight into unlocking hidden commercial potential within individuals who are working in organisations but who are not currently employed in a sales role. The book is written both for (future) technical experts and the people leaders who manage them.

HR departments have to make assumptions about the needs, aspirations and capabilities of different groups of people in the organisation and look for scalable and standardised processes and/or tools to help develop and transform skills to realise the business growth objectives. Unfortunately, most current approaches and technologies do not help people understand their commercial potential or see in which type of context they can unlock that potential.

Rather than assuming what the needs are of non-sales employees in one given organisation, my goal is to understand commercial potential from multiple angles. To achieve this, I conducted international research in 2023 to understand the drivers of commercial impact and potential of technical experts using my two models COSMOS and AIM with 536 employees **currently not working in a sales role**.[4] The respondents spanned twelve countries and a variety of industries, roles and levels of seniority.

For all of these people, I also collected their employee experience data, insights into personal value drivers and personality characteristics using three types of scientific models and tools.[5] Throughout the book, I will cover the most relevant conclusions of that research. In addition to understanding drivers of commercial impact via these three surveys, I asked a few specific questions to all the participants in the study. Here are some interesting findings to get us started:

- Of the people surveyed, 85% get professional satisfaction from contributing to commercial success, and 81% like to help solve business problems for a customer. This confirms that many employees would be willing to discuss how they can add a commercial aspect to their role.

- Of all respondents, 44% state their commercial potential is underused, so most organisations are not yet tapping into the full potential of their employees or aware of the fact that employees are interested in expanding their roles in such directions. What is blocking these individuals from unlocking more of their commercial potential?

In this book, I will share the personality traits and values of non-salespeople that can be leveraged to unlock that potential. I will also uncover which boosters or blockers could potentially help to unlock more commercial performance and development.

Selling in a complex business-to-business (B2B) environment is all about selling a new idea that helps a customer reach a better outcome than where they are now – in other words, improve their situation – and I will look at research which confirms that aiming for customer improvement is the surest way to client retention and growth. The key concept of customer improvement is more likely to be seen as having a higher purpose and can appeal to a larger group of job profiles than the idea of product or solution growth or sales targets.

Using long-term customer improvement as a key purpose can have real impact when unlocking individual commercial potential. It could become the litmus test for new commercial business models and ideas. We can all think of several business models which will have to be revisited if we are to keep our planet liveable and offer a sustainable future for generations to come, but who can come up with new customer improvement ideas and how can we inspire people to act on these? What are the perceived barriers at the individual and organisational levels? Selling and implementing customer improvement in organisations doesn't seem that simple in today's complex world.

The surveyed respondents state that they don't know how to sell or mobilise people to act on their ideas. This is not easy because we all have different individual experiences, mindsets and perspectives, so what works for one person may not work for someone else. I will share the perspectives of the respondents on their perceived boosters or blockers of commercial potential, asking how much of this has to do with the support of direct managers.

The good news is that over 82% of the respondents say their manager is supportive of commercial capability development. When respondents are asked, however, for what reason they are not able to convince people of the relevance of their customer improvement ideas, they often report that their line managers do not believe it is something they need to be focused on. Customer improvement ideas often span different functions, but if every function is focused on delivering on the manager's own priorities it is difficult to get great ideas implemented. The problem is that most ideas for customer improvement require cross-function collaboration. As one respondent simply puts it: 'Customer improvement ideas don't get implemented because there is organisational apathy.'

Two models for change

How do we break silos and enable all types of experts in an organisation to anticipate needs, to inspire different stakeholders with new insight and to mobilise change by rallying people in different departments around new customer improvement ideas? I call this having a commercial **AIM**: **A**nticipate needs, **I**nspire with insight, **M**obilise change. The commercial framework (called **COSMOS**) in Part Two can be used as a checklist to prepare for commercial impact. It can be applied straight away to help increase commercial impact and outcomes at an individual, group or organisational level, especially in B2B contexts. AIM describes the mindset and behaviours that, if combined and put into action, will support customer improvement through implementing the COSMOS framework.

By using both AIM (to drive customer improvement) and COSMOS (as a preparation framework for specific opportunities) for all customer interactions, technical experts will be able to make a noticeable impact on the client experience. As a result, they will also help create opportunities to improve client retention and increase business growth.

The COSMOS framework applies to every commercial context, independent of the size or type of the organisation you work for or the products and services your organisation sells. It can also easily be used as a preparation tool alongside different sales and delivery methodologies to impact customer improvement at every stage of the sales or delivery process. This framework will help technical experts to be less reliant on the knowledge or expertise of salespeople and take ownership of commercial skill development. The reward for this effort is being more employable and able to demonstrate skills needed in the future.

Why should we care about changing the approach in organisations to hire and develop sales talent? Quite simply, because there is a substantial opportunity cost linked to not changing our current approaches, as illustrated by my survey. Of the respondents:

- 54% state that their customer improvement ideas that weren't implemented could have led to **positive environmental impact**

- 62% state that their customer improvement ideas that weren't implemented could have led to **revenue increase**

- 65% state that their customer improvement ideas that weren't implemented could have led to **cost savings**

- 67% state that their customer improvement ideas that weren't implemented could have led to **time savings**

- 67% state that their customer improvement ideas that weren't implemented could have had a **positive people impact** (engagement, wellbeing etc)

We need to become more agile and turn such ideas into tangible outcomes, while offering the right insights for individuals and leaders in organisations. Of the respondents, 51% agree with the following statement: 'If I had a better understanding of how I could drive and support commercial outcomes, I would have a bigger impact in my organisation.'

In this book, I will look at the individual employee experiences, personality traits and value drivers, and some leadership characteristics and approaches, which may be conducive to the development of commercial capability in organisations. I will also touch on how AI and technology should be key components of an organisational transition towards seizing a higher amount of commercial opportunities. The book contains practical tips and frameworks to drive a positive people, business and environmental impact.

All the concepts shared in this book can be adopted by individuals and teams alongside what the organisation is already doing; the book is agnostic on a specific sales model or stage of the sales or delivery process.

I will go so far as to claim that even seasoned sales professionals will find this book a helpful refresher of what it takes to drive commercial impact.

My goal is to empower every employee and leader with a framework to help them focus on their commercial capability development skills and, as a result, be more successful in impacting business growth.

PART ONE
CUSTOMER IMPROVEMENT SELLING: THE CASE FOR CHANGE

The first three chapters of the book will provide an overview of and background to why a case for change to customer improvement selling is now, more than ever, relevant to consider for technical experts and organisations. In Chapter 1 I will clarify how I define a technical expert and review the difference between commercial skills, capabilities and potential, then look at how we can measure those qualities. I will end this chapter with understanding the factors that limit the development of commercial capabilities for technical experts.

In Chapter 2 I will discuss the evolution of sales and buying approaches in a complex B2B context, as well as the challenges sales teams have been facing. Some fascinating research surfaced in recent years which deserves our attention.

In Chapter 3 I will debunk a couple of myths which make it difficult for technical experts to drive towards customer improvement and business growth. I will also cover how technical experts can play a key role in driving growth by aligning to critical buyer expectations and, more importantly, even proactively shaping the buyer agenda.

1

Why Technical Experts Need Commercial Capabilities In The Twenty-First Century

Commercial capabilities are critical if businesses are to thrive. Organisations will always need people who are adept at selling goods or services. This is especially true in a more complex B2B sales context. 'Complex' doesn't refer to the complexity of the product or service a company sells but to the number of stakeholders involved in the purchasing decision, to the long sales cycle and to the higher number of meetings required to close a sale.

Although not every employee will have to become a salesperson, almost all employees should develop some degree of commercial skilfulness. This means that every employee should have some understanding of how customers respond to products and services and how specific behaviours and activities can lead to customer growth or retention. Products, services and processes can change rapidly. Having employees with strong commercial capabilities in the organisation will ensure that businesses stay aware of the challenges to their business models. Awareness can then lead to a successful adaptation of the business model to the new context.

Society is changing faster than ever before. Digitalisation has had consequences for many traditional industries (media, music, advertising). Disruption is happening everywhere we look and there is no sign of it slowing down. If anything, the COVID-19 pandemic showed how quickly business models (the entertainment, hospitality and health and fitness industries) can be at risk of becoming obsolete. What does that predict for a future in which global warming becomes a larger issue? Think of the future for the fossil fuels industry, the aviation sector and producers of combustion engines. Many organisations whose business models have become outdated are struggling, and the future looks uncertain for many more.

There is more at stake than can be solved by developing new products and services. Leaders must come up with a clear rationale, or return on investment (ROI) formula, on why commercial partnerships with other organisations should be renewed. When the economic climate is uncertain, tangible proof needs to be provided that a new contract won't add unnecessary financial risks or costs to a business. The absence of such proof can mean that commercial partnerships may be paused for an undefined period, or even stopped altogether.

When new investments are scrutinised by professional procurement teams because belts are being tightened, leaders are forced to think differently about how they can keep their core activities running or grow commercial partnerships.

Fortunately, in most organisations the front-line sales teams have extensive opportunities to learn more about new sales and buyer processes and behaviours. They participate in numerous sales training courses to increase the likelihood of being more effective at selling or driving value for new and existing customers.

Focusing development investments on sales teams makes logical sense because every dollar spent on increasing the skills of salespeople can have an immediate impact on business results and commercial relationships, but we need to do more. Of those surveyed in my international research group (of people *not* currently employed in a sales role), 54% say that that no commercial capability development at all is offered to them on a yearly basis.

Commercial skills are now considered to be an essential characteristic of a successful twenty-first century workforce. The COVID-19 outbreak confirmed the need for this shift. Organisations that have designed and embedded robust processes to select, develop and retain employees with strong commercial capability will have a key competitive advantage in the years to come.

A closer look at technical experts

In this book I want to focus on a specific group of employees: technical experts. I will challenge the assumption that technical experts don't need to be too involved in commercial activities or think about their role in growing or retaining commercial relationships.

What is a technical expert? In the context of this book, it is anyone who can (directly or indirectly) shape a commercial experience by contributing with their expertise at a specific moment in the sales process to support the scoping and closing of the sale of a solution in a B2B sales context.

Professionals who are part of the delivery of the solution (eg those involved in implementation, data and training, usage consultants and experts) can therefore be technical experts. Technical experts may also be people who have chosen a profession which has nothing to do with sales (eg accounting, engineering, law experts, HR) but who need to get involved in selling to progress to the next step in a career.

If the definition of a technical expert applies to you, where are you on this matrix?

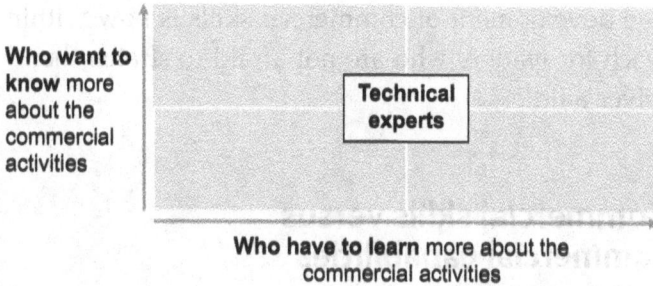

Who want to know more about the commercial activities

Technical experts

Who have to learn more about the commercial activities

Need and want to learn about commercial activities?

Apart from people in the bottom left corner (technical experts who don't want to know and don't have to learn more about commercial activities), this book will offer insights and tools to increase commercial impact for all (future) technical experts.

Technical experts are managed by people leaders who can play a key role in motivating and coaching towards improved commercial awareness and impact. I will combine sales with HR management science and offer insights into the key ingredients for leaders to effectively coach towards behaviour change, which will help drive commercial and personal impact.

Technical experts who understand COSMOS can start applying their commercial AIM within the context of their current jobs. They can build on the technical knowledge they already have and work with the

17

people in their companies while adding value to their businesses.

The development of commercial skills is now within reach for readers who are not afraid to stretch themselves a little.

Commercial skills versus commercial capabilities

After working for over two decades in the human capital industry, I have realised that the majority of people use words such as 'skills' and 'capabilities' interchangeably to define similar concepts. A relevant description I found to describe the difference between skill and capability is from Neil Tambe:

> 'A **skill** is something you learn to do and go do it. [...] A **capability** isn't a specific **skill** that fits in a given situation. It's a deep-rooted **ability** which can be applied in many contexts. It's something you train and have to learn to do in context.'[6]

Let's take this definition and zoom in on commercial skills versus commercial capabilities. A **commercial** or **sales skill** could be, for example, negotiation skills, objection handling or sales presentation skills. There are proven strategies which can help you improve these. Becoming proficient in a sales skill takes an average of thirteen days compared to an average of fifty-nine days for any of the other skills on the top skills list for the future.[7] The list also includes skills such as data management and machine learning. These are, of course, a lot harder to become skilled at than commercial skills: they require more time, new abstract knowledge and (in most cases) an expensive traditional learning context.

Commercial capability is involved in developing these commercial skills, but it refers to the ability to understand and behave successfully throughout a variety of different approaches and contexts which can positively impact commercial outcomes. It is not limited to people who are participating in a sales process or focusing on the act of selling a product or a service. Instead, it is about the behaviours and mindset you need to have to flexibly adopt different frameworks, tools and approaches so that you can align and tailor to the needs of the specific context and aim for your highest potential impact on customer growth and retention.

This book will help build the commercial capability of technical experts by focusing on key behaviours and a framework which can maximise the impact someone can have on improving customer outcomes, such as growth and retention in different organisational contexts and roles.

What is commercial potential and can we measure it?

The difference between **potential** and **capability** can be explained using a simple analogy: commercial capability should be observable by stakeholders around you. For example: during a meeting you have inspired a customer stakeholder to take a different action, which helps them realise the need to move towards a new outcome. This was a result of successful preparation and of providing them with a surprising insight which taps into the key customer context, concerns and needs.

Commercial potential is not what you can observe (eg someone's actions or behaviours); it is invisible, but it will influence how and why someone will likely behave in a way that is aligned to expectations in a given role or context.

Commercial potential consists of the following elements:

- **Working style preferences**: personality traits which indicate, for example, someone's preferred approach to solving customer problems and working with other people to leverage information and knowledge, looking at the broader, long-term context or developing a new game plan

- **Motivation and value drivers**: different intrinsic and extrinsic levers which provide energy and ownership for participating in commercial contributions and / or learning new relevant skills and approaches to mobilise internal and external behaviour change

- **The capacity to deal with more connected and/ or complex topics potentially outside of one's technical domain**: the world of the customer and links between what's happening in the market and what could happen in a customer organisation as a result

All the components of potential will influence the choices someone makes and the actions and behaviours they display. These choices and actions may or may not align to expectations of a team or customer.

Technical knowledge and commercial skills can be measured in different ways. There are many available tests and approaches to certify whether someone can put commercial theory into practice on the job. Testing acquired technical knowledge or skills can be relevant but has its limits, and it certainly does not predict future commercial behaviour.

For example, to drive a car you need both theoretical knowledge and practical skills. A thorough understanding of traffic rules as well as the ability to drive will earn someone their licence. The driving test, however, can provide only a picture of retained information at the moment of the exam. It ticks the box of acquired knowledge – at that moment. It does not predict how safely someone will drive a car in the future nor how quickly and willingly someone will learn and adapt their driving style to new rules.

There are ways to predict commercial behaviour by looking, for example, at someone's underlying personality style, working style preferences, motivation and values. These traits and characteristics remain relatively stable, and measuring them gives direction to someone's likely approach in the future in a given context. Going back to the car example, a typical value or personality trait or preference could be around conformity to rules (individual value dimension) and inclination to be rule-following (personality trait).[8]

Psychometric workplace diagnostics or assessments can be applied to help make these invisible traits (or someone's potential to behave in a certain way in a work context) visible. It can help describe values and working style preferences which help to understand someone's commercial potential. As you will read in this book, predictive psychometric assessments are not often used for technical experts to uncover barriers and/or future opportunities in relation to their commercial potential, because it is not deemed necessary. By understanding these invisible characteristics, however, we can help unlock someone's potential to apply behaviours which can drive commercial impact. We will cover these specific behaviours in more detail later.

Commercial potential can be measured in a predictive way using validated and proven psychometric workplace questionnaires such as on working style preference, motivational drivers, and values. The most modern workplace assessments are administered online and sold by test providers who adhere to different occupational psychology theories. Predictive assessment tools will help to predict commercial behaviours and report on areas of strength, risk or development opportunity in a role or context.

Many internationally used psychometric assessments have been around for a long time, but they have not changed much in that time. To review the impact of commercial potential on technical experts, I conducted my research by evaluating the responses against a personality questionnaire and a well-known international individual values framework by Prof Schwartz.[9] More information on the linkages between these models and the frameworks offered can be found in Chapter 14.

Well-constructed and validated psychometric assessments can reduce risk and enable growth for both individuals and organisations and help to make sure that no hidden potential is wasted. Every organisation could assess the commercial potential of their workforce to determine where they stand and whether incorporating new development strategies might be beneficial to the longer-term success of the organisation. These tools also help individuals to become more self-aware – a quality which is foundational to helping employees take ownership of their personal development and destiny.

Any change involving learning a new skill or behaviour starts with self-awareness: where I am now and what I should be reinforcing (or mindful of) to be even more successful. Organisations with employees who are more self-aware have stronger financial performance than organisations with workforces that are less self-aware.[10] A research study that included more than 5,000 respondents uncovered that although 95% of leaders think they're self-aware, only 10–15% truly are.[11] We can safely assume that people in non-leadership roles who have been exposed less to developmental capability programmes will have even lower levels of self-insight.

This piece of the people puzzle related to commercial potential is crucial information for business leaders to coach effectively and make investment decisions in the area of development, recruitment and succession for technical expert roles (not just for leadership and commercial roles). Every change initiative required to deal with increased complexity and the design or implementation of a new business strategy will fail if the people in the organisation don't have the means to understand what it takes to execute it. The good news? Any technical expert can start to initiate their change journey after reading this book.

Limiting factors

Even if the case for the development of commercial capabilities of technical experts is clear, many companies don't invest in it. Why don't we see a structural shift in the way commercial capabilities are being developed and aligned to the latest changes in commercial and behavioural best practices? It is because we have built too many silos in our organisations. These silos can have competing objectives and priorities and therefore hinder each other's development. To seize the opportunity of creating a more commercially minded and capable workforce, we need to break through several types of silos.

The division of development and upskilling across the workforce

Sales teams often get access to fancy offsite events, kick-offs and sales training, while the rest of the business has to be satisfied with a few slides that summarise the commercial learnings, delivered by their functional executive or a representative who was able to attend these sessions. We cannot assume commercial capability (or the investment in developing commercial capability) in organisations is needed only for people in sales, finance-related or leadership positions. Less than half of the technical experts get access to commercial capability development (defined in survey as best practices in how to drive customer outcomes such as growth and loyalty, skill development to be more effective in selling a new idea to different customer stakeholders),… but in 76% of the cases it is focused on the company strategy and goals, the product and solution impact on customers and the processes and tools needed to be successful in driving impact. Only 22% of their commercial development training is focused on understanding the required behaviours to be successful in driving commercial impact.

How much time is invested in your commercial capability development per year*? (n=536)

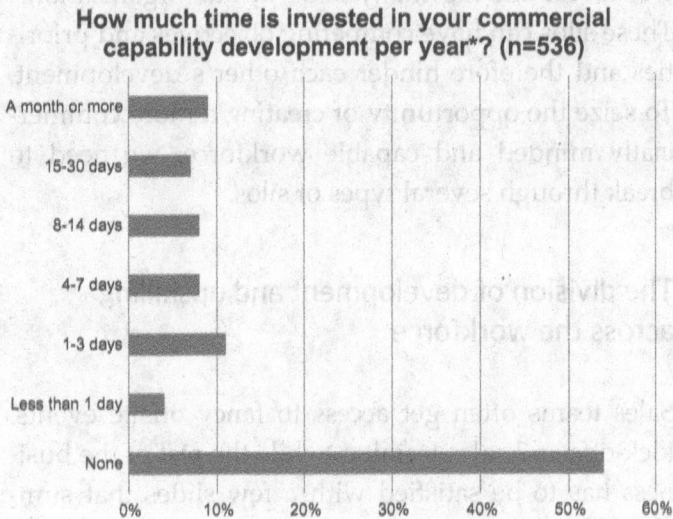

Time invested in commercial capability development per year by percentage of respondents (employees currently not in a sales role)[12]

According to the Future of Jobs Report in 2023, the highest priority for skills training from 2023 to 2027 is analytical thinking, followed by creative thinking. Both are set to account for 8–10% of upskilling initiatives, on average.[13] The risk with current upskilling approaches is that these are often tackled in isolation and/or approached from within business silos.

Today's customer-first digital business models require employees in every position to be aware of (and focused on) their impact on the bottom line of their own company as well as the business impact they have on the customers they serve. Those technical experts who are not in sales but who do have a key delivery role in front of the customer are often forgotten in commercial development activities. A better commercial alignment and understanding of what it takes to drive commercial impact, especially for technical experts or employees impacting the client delivery or buying process, can play a huge role in a company's success.

Sales and technical expert teams may not be aligned

In the best-case scenario, technical experts are brought in to support the sales cycle and shape the best solution for the customer. This is not always the case, as in many organisations technical experts play a role only once the solution is sold, for instance to deliver the project. They have to deliver what has been sold by salespeople who may not have scoped the right solution as seen through the eyes of the technical expert or who may not have detected the solution with the best long-term outcomes. When technical experts engage with the client without much context or a deeper diagnosis on why a specific solution or implementation was chosen, they have no choice but to rely on only their own technical expertise.

Salespeople often forget that technical experts can sometimes have more access to senior stakeholders and get listened to because they are not in a formal sales setting. Technical experts also take pride in sharing their expertise and helping to solve problems. Why does their expertise not always lead to new commercial opportunities? Partly because sales is not their core discipline and they often miss the commercial fundamentals or understanding of the behaviours that lead to success or the broader context to successfully navigate towards new commercial opportunities.

The way sales and technical experts are incentivised may even lead to competing outcomes. The salesperson may want to sign a more transactional deal before the end of the month, while a technical expert or delivery person advises that a different solution may be better for the longer-term success of the client. The quick win may impact sales bonus recognition in a way which stimulates behaviour that doesn't lead to the longer-term client outcomes.

If priorities are competing, it can be an uphill battle to strive for longer-term customer improvement. It takes experience and assertiveness for commercially minded technical experts to paddle against the stream and drive commercial opportunities to a close. Proactively partnering with sales colleagues to drive longer-term client value and going beyond the described tasks, while often not even getting formally recognised for this work, takes a strong commercial mindset and resilience. I will elaborate more on the specific personality traits and values in Part Three.

Exposing employees to only research and best practices of their own functional domain

New sales or buyer research and best practices will be relevant to chief commercial officers and their sales teams. New best practices on how to coach team members, improve employee experience and engagement or change human behaviour to have a long-lasting effect will appeal mostly to stakeholders in HR Management and learning and development teams. Who is connecting the dots? Someone should. It makes logical sense to combine the learnings and best practice insights of both functional disciplines and make these easily available and understood for everyone in the business to learn from. We are more likely to see new skills or behaviours adopted and embedded if we understand hidden potential and which boosters and blockers may stand in the way of unlocking this potential.

Aligning efforts and communication on functional initiatives where there is a joint outcome to be achieved would mean that the launched initiatives don't compete for the same scarce time or attention of the field teams. To break this silo, we have to spend more time and effort on clearly aligning and communicating how best practice commercial approaches and frameworks go hand in hand with behavioural change best practices. All employees and their leaders need to understand why they should pay attention to connecting the learnings of both and embedding these in their day-to-day routine to drive improved business and personal value.

Of the respondents in my international research sample of non-salespeople, 35% believe there is no intentional best practice sharing beyond one's own functional domain, and another 28% are unsure of the intentions of sharing across domains, which means if we are sharing cross-functional best practices, we need to do a better job at communicating the purpose.[14]

How many technical experts reading this book have proactively been offered opportunities to develop core commercial capabilities, whether on the job or somewhere else?

Many HR experts and corporate learning and development specialists do not yet see their roles as enablers of commercial capabilities outside of sales. It is seen as a responsibility for the sales or sales enablement function. In the same way, chief commercial officers focus too much on chasing numbers and investing in product training, process and technology improvements. They do not always realise that change programmes focusing on customer improvement can boost numbers through a different approach.

Incentivising collaboration across the silos will be a key priority for everyone in the organisation. Businesses have many opportunities to collaborate more to ensure that individuals have the time, motivation and means to seek commercial development opportunities.

Keeping valuable predictive insight within recruitment

Psychometric workplace assessments help reduce risk for both individuals and organisations and avoid hidden potential being wasted. Using psychometric assessments uncovers gaps in understanding and offers a solid basis for a discussion about someone's role and approach to better impact and seize customer improvement opportunities. It can also focus the forward-looking development or performance discussion on questions such as 'What can I achieve?', as we will cover in more detail in Part Three.

Many of the psychometric workplace assessments report against different behavioural frameworks and offer predictive insight into the potential for change at the individual, team or organisational level, usually with a key role in mind. Organisations rarely look, however, beyond the immediate role and forget to measure what someone is capable of when given free rein in a context that offers the opportunity to impact different customers and outcomes.

Many technical experts are still hired without predictive psychometric workplace assessments. Recruiters too often rely on data in CVs, technical capabilities and past performance or experience, with little attention given to the candidate's commercial potential, especially if the role has no immediate commercial responsibility. Of course, the primary focus for a hiring process needs to be on looking for the best candidate fit to the role, but if two technical expert candidates are similar but one has strong commercial potential and the other does not, then the choice should be for the former candidate.

A wrong hire can result in frustration, a waste of money and a waste of resources. These costs far outweigh the investment needed to use psychometric tools. Even in more forward-looking organisations that already incorporate assessments in recruitment processes, the predictive information is rarely used for further development or other purposes which may help to uncover the full commercial potential.

A predictive workplace assessment applied in a recruitment setting can, however, be (re)used to explore and develop commercial potential for existing employees as well. Nevertheless, few organisations apply the same rigour when it comes to making important career decisions for internal personnel.

Strategic decisions and change decisions are still too often made only on the basis of financial data and gut feeling. Data on someone's past performance alone cannot help us to increase commercial capability in teams and the organisation.

Organisations should assess the commercial potential of their workforce to determine where they stand and whether incorporating new strategies might be beneficial to longer-term success. This is crucial information for business leaders to make investment decisions in the area of development and to recruit and plan succession for technical expert roles (not just for leadership and commercial roles). As we have seen, offering deeper and more accurate self-insight is critical to helping people take ownership of their career and development.

2

The Sales And Buying Evolution

The world of B2B sales and buying has evolved dramatically in the last two decades. In the next section we will cover different sales approaches and explore the important features in the world of buying.

A variety of sales approaches

Customer improvement selling has become the most effective and recession-proof sales approach and consistently leads to more sales productivity and better business performance. The figure below shows three different approaches I will discuss in this chapter, and examples of conversation openers.

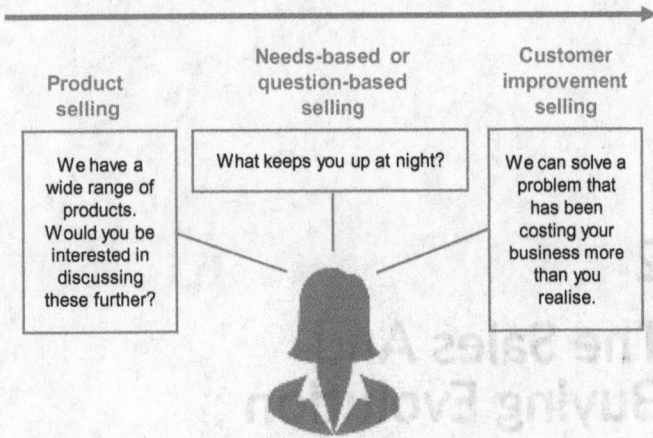

Product selling	Needs-based or question-based selling	Customer improvement selling
We have a wide range of products. Would you be interested in discussing these further?	What keeps you up at night?	We can solve a problem that has been costing your business more than you realise.

Sales conversation starters – from product selling to customer improvement selling

Product selling

Product selling used to be a more popular choice than it is today. It means that the salesperson leads the commercial interaction with details and information about their products and services, and with unique differentiators. The value for the client is created through the product and the way it is positioned against the price of comparable products or services in the market. The time investment for the client in a product-selling approach is minimal because they listen to what the salesperson has to offer and it quickly becomes clear whether there is a needs match with the product or service and whether specific product features are relevant to solve a specific client problem.

To present the products and services, technical experts or salespeople need to be well versed in explaining relevant features. In this sales process, the product itself is key to winning the deal. When products are similar in the eyes of the clients, the logical next question is who offers the best value for money. As a result, professional procurement teams became more actively involved in the sales process, to shield the customers from salespeople and to ensure objective and clear price comparisons.

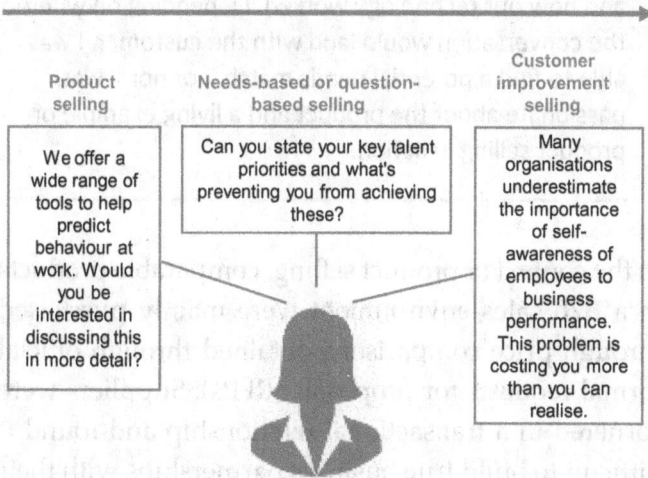

Product selling	Needs-based or question-based selling	Customer improvement selling
We offer a wide range of tools to help predict behaviour at work. Would you be interested in discussing this in more detail?	Can you state your key talent priorities and what's preventing you from achieving these?	Many organisations underestimate the importance of self-awareness of employees to business performance. This problem is costing you more than you can realise.

Sales conversation starters – a salesperson selling HR assessment tools

REFLECTION: PRODUCT SELLING IN ACTION

Fresh from university in 2000, I started my career as an HR consultant. Although a consulting role was more of a technical role, selling our products and services was part of the job description because there was no separate sales function. On my first day I was handed a pile of product brochures to read. There were no bite-sized e-learning modules or sales onboarding programmes yet. This meant I had to figure it out on my own. Without any formal sales training, it seemed logical to learn both the features of our own products and services and those of our competitors.

My main sales aids were my laptop, full of sample tests, and several product brochures. These helped me to show which products could be relevant to a customer and how our technology worked. Depending on where the conversation would land with the customer, I was able to find a potential needs match... or not. I was passionate about the product and a living example of product selling in action.

In the context of product selling, comparable products in a B2B sales environment were mainly purchased through price comparisons obtained through official formal requests for proposals (RFPs). Suppliers were cornered in a transactional relationship and found it difficult to build true business partnerships with their customers.

Product selling still exists today: salespeople can choose to talk predominantly about the products or services they want to sell. It is the simplest form of selling, but it has proven challenging to maintain healthy profit margins. In today's context, product selling remains commercially interesting only for those companies who can offer the products and services on a large scale. They can offer competitive prices based on high sales volumes.

Needs-based selling

Needs-based selling (also called question-based selling) uses an open-ended needs analysis to lead to commercial interactions. It is all about a salesperson asking questions designed to get the customer to articulate their business needs and then becoming a trusted advisor. The salesperson must tie the customer's needs back to single products or services, or to an existing bundle or solution to solve the client issue.

The challenge with this approach lies in the fact that technical experts need to be involved early in the sales process because it is difficult to predict in which direction the client will focus the conversation. Contrary to the product-selling approach, where the client's time investment is minimal, in the needs-based selling approach the customers spend a lot of time explaining their unique context and priorities.

REFLECTION: NEEDS-BASED SELLING

My first proper sales training was focused on understanding the sales process and how to use different questioning techniques in a needs-based sales conversation. Many sales companies have invested a lot of time and money in training salespeople in these techniques. To help salespeople ask the right questions in the right order. Salespeople use active listening skills to eventually funnel to a needs match with what the organisation can offer.

I have seen many salespeople over-engineer their questioning approach after this type of sales training. Although there is a time and place in customer conversations for good diagnosis of needs, skilful questioning and keeping a two-way dialogue going, without losing sight of the outcome, can be difficult. If the salesperson is too focused on what they want to get out of the meeting, the needs of the customer will not get enough attention. Clients have busy schedules and are usually short on people and resources. The last thing they want is to lose an entire hour in a sales meeting and learn nothing new. A client meeting focused on information gathering by the salesperson can easily result in a frustrating client experience if the client does not learn new insights.

If customers are sharing all the context factors and unique business needs and priorities, an expectation is created that at the end of this conversation there will be a customised solution designed to meet their unique needs. To add value in the meeting and be a partner in jointly solving the challenges of the customer, salespeople almost always need a technical expert present.

In this sales approach both the scoping and delivery of the solution are difficult. The solution will be shaped based on how the client defines their needs and sometimes using a limited level of diagnosis skills. Solutions scoped following a needs-based selling approach often become too complex or too customised to deliver. High customisation requirements based on unique client requests are often not (fully) covered in the fees paid by the client and put pressure on internal teams, standard delivery processes and margins.

When a more bespoke solution gets sold, it is likely to be coupled with a lengthy implementation, and the client becomes the guinea pig for an untested solution without a guarantee of or link to improved business outcomes. The value in this needs-based selling approach is mostly created through customisation of the product and/or services.

This type of selling was once the dominant sales approach driven by suppliers who wanted to move out of commoditised transactional product selling. For many years, the deal complexity went up in alignment with the customer's natural desire to customise. By default, this made the sales approach and the delivery of the solution costly for organisations, who had to double their resources in almost all steps of the sales process. At the end, they delivered an expensive and unscalable customised solution. Technical experts would sometimes be doing the selling work, and sales would just set up the meetings and do the administrative work to secure the contract.

Customer improvement selling

In the aftermath of the global financial crisis, CEB Inc, now part of Gartner®, launched one of the most important sales productivity studies to answer a question that many organisations were struggling with. Which sales type and approach is recession-proof and leads to consistent sales performance and improved customer outcomes? Based on an exhaustive study of thousands of sales reps across multiple industries and geographies, the research arm of CEB Inc, The Sales Executive Council, defined Challenger® selling as a new sales approach.[15,16]

Unfortunately, if you don't dive into the detail of the philosophy behind this sales approach (which C-level leaders don't always do), it may sound like your main goal is to 'challenge' a customer, which sounds contradictory to customer-centric strategies. A different name for this new type of selling came from another school of thought, where this sales approach was called 'insight selling'. This term was first introduced by Mike Schultz.[17] Rather than looking at the salespeople, researchers looked at the buyer side of the equation. The issue with this label is, again, that when judging the cover by its title and not diving into the detail, it seems the trick to success is using insight. 'Insight' is, however, such a broad and overused term that it may not be tied to the customer's needs. Following my own research, in which 81% of technical experts confirm they like to solve business problems of customers, the need for alignment of technical experts to relevant B2B sales and buyer best practices and the points I am making, I want to continue calling this third sales philosophy on the evolution spectrum 'customer improvement selling'.

In this third type of selling, a Challenger salesperson leads commercial interactions with insights, as opposed to leading with product offerings or a needs analysis. This approach helps to challenge assumptions in the client's thinking and exposes the flaws in their way of seeing a customer problem. The next step is to present a better course of action, which can lead to improved customer outcomes. The value from this sales approach is achieved through realising the competitive advantage.

The goal in this approach is to teach a client something new, which can help to solve a sizeable problem they may not have been aware of. To be successful in this type of conversation, a powerful commercial insight, or teaching message, needs to be prepared to help the customer think differently and take action.

This type of approach to sales is more likely to help salespeople get ahead of a new RFP, because they are in a position to create a new need entirely based on a unique perspective that can help a client reach better business outcomes. This is a far better position to be in than either having to fulfil a well-defined existing need from a client you have not spoken to before or receiving a detailed product or service request and a spreadsheet to complete with product pricing.

COVID-19 has forced organisations to consider completely new ways of doing business, and a looming recession will confirm that organisations who have embedded customer improvement selling approaches in their sales process will likely be more successful than those who have stayed in the needs-based selling approach. Why? Not only is customer improvement selling a more predictive path to commercial success, but also its costs of sales and delivery are lower than those for needs-based selling. Companies using needs-based selling have to double the costs of resources to drive highly customised solutions presented by salespeople with the help of technical experts.

All businesses are interested in different and unique perspectives on how they can do business in a more effective way and reduce risks. When organisations are in survival mode there is a burning platform which forces them to look for a new course of action to keep the business running.

A commercial interaction must be valuable for both parties, and this can happen only if a tailored insight message has been prepared. This approach moves beyond selling a product. It involves selling a promise of achieving competitive advantage through customer or business improvement. With an abundance of information available on the internet or through user groups, preparing an effective commercial teaching message means connecting pieces of information in a unique way so that the client will sit up and take notice.

What about selling solutions?

Selling products or services in a pure transactional approach was leading to increasing commoditisation processes. As a response, organisations created new bundles or packages of products and services (solution offerings), which were more difficult for competitors to replicate. Packaged solutions have the additional advantage that they are tried and tested and more likely to have a proven link to business outcomes. Effectively packaged solutions or bundles of products and services can be sold using different sales approaches.

The link between customer improvement and client growth and retention

Loyalty research conducted by Corporate Executive Board (CEB), now Gartner, measured customer loyalty with three questions. First, will a customer come back to you for more of your products and services? Second, will they refer you to other customers? Third, would they be open to buying additional new services from you? The factor with the highest impact on driving customer loyalty came from the sales experience. In this same research the voice of the customer, a great sales experience is created by a sales rep who:

- Offers me unique, valuable perspectives on my market

- Helps me navigate alternatives

- Provides ongoing advice or consultation

- Helps me avoid potential risks

- Educates me on new issues and outcomes

- Is easy to buy from

- Has widespread support in my organisation

The sales experience has as much as 53% impact on customer loyalty, compared to 47% for other factors combined (Company and Brand 19%, Product and Service Delivery 19% and Value-to-price ratio 9%).[18]

This finding has been widely debated but feels empowering for anyone impacting the sales experience, because as a salesperson interacts with customers, they can adapt their approach to different buyers. The sales experience that is created has more impact on the client than the product or the company/brand the salesperson works for. Put differently, *how* someone sells is more important than *what* someone sells. Any of the three sales approaches outlined in this chapter can be chosen, regardless of an organisation's preferred sales philosophy. The approach of leading with products, questions or customer improvement insight can also be applied or reinforced by anyone who has a role to play in the entire sales and delivery process.

A closer look at the buyer context

Considering the statistics discussed earlier in the chapter, it is helpful to ask why it isn't enough to focus on the sales teams. For what reasons would internal teams and technical experts need to support the already successful approach of customer improvement selling? The answer is related to today's buying context, in which selling is often done in a team, with some people in the front office and some in the back office. They all impact the sales experience and opportunity. Technical experts can play an important role in helping salespeople prepare for optimal impact and commercial success, because of the characteristics of this new buyer context.

Buying analysis paralysis

Buying solutions or products in a complex B2B environment has become really challenging. When customers want to buy something, the internet provides an abundance of information. Reviews and comparisons of different products, services and their corresponding features can all be found online. Buyers get access to more alternatives and options as new technologies, products, suppliers and services emerge. There is too much information and too many options.

On average it now takes six to ten different stakeholders to make a purchase decision in a complex B2B selling context.[19] Each of the stakeholders involved in the process is armed with four or five pieces of information that they have gathered independently and must 'deconflict' with the group. Reaching an agreement with so many different views and pieces of information would be a challenging task even for experts in conflict resolution, so imagine the uphill battle for stakeholders who have no background in facilitation or consensus building.

At around 37% completion of a complex B2B buying journey, a typical buying group throws in the towel because they are unable to reach a consensus on the business problem and/or the way to solve it.[20] At this point the buyer group has failed to reach consensus. It is not a situation salespeople can solve by themselves; they are probably not even aware a buying journey has started. They will need the help of technical experts to influence and sell change more widely and more effectively. We will cover this in more detail in Chapter 3.

Suppliers are involved only when the brief is ready

If the buyers get past their conflicting views and reach a consensus on a possible solution for a business problem, which happens at around 57% completion of the buying journey, they are ready to get input from potential suppliers.[21] The more complex the deal, the later they will engage with suppliers. This means more than half of the journey has been made without the buyer ever meeting with a supplier. According to a 2018 Gartner report, when B2B buyers were considering a purchase, they spent only 17% of that time meeting with potential suppliers, and that amount needed to be divided evenly across multiple suppliers.[22]

When a buyer is comparing providers, the amount of time spent with any one sales representative may be only 5% or 6% of the time of the total buying journey.[23] Salespeople have a lot less influence on customer decisions these days. There is only a small window of opportunity to make an impact, so the meeting needs to be pitch-perfect. Often there is no second chance. It requires thorough preparation of a strong commercial teaching message and the anticipation of stakeholder needs and motivators. These activities are more likely to lead to success when technical experts are involved to add a different perspective.

It takes a village to buy

In the past, salespeople were fishing for a big catch: airtime with the people in the most senior buying roles to convince them to buy a new product or solution. Today, not even a stellar meeting with the most senior person who has the authority to sign will be sufficient. Why? The senior economic buyer will be interested in whether the supplier has widespread support across their organisation, and this buy-in is more important than the solution they will buy. Buyers have become more risk-averse over the years and will not take a purchase decision alone; they want to spread the risk. Every opinion matters, not just the opinion of the people with the power to sign or who are the highest in rank.

Two new challenges have therefore surfaced: reaching a consensus with so many different stakeholders and perspectives, and mobilising people towards change. The problem is that a sales representative does not necessarily understand the power structures in the organisation. They will need to find a person to rely on to navigate this buying network and facilitate a consensus in favour of acquiring a new product or solution. In Part Two we will look at how to identify such people and how to work with them to achieve your goal.

Buyer indecision

Human beings have deep-seated bias for things to remain as they are. We have an aversion to change. A global piece of research based on analysing millions of sales interactions concluded that between 40% and 60% of deals today end up stalled in 'no decision' limbo.[24] The customers are indecisive about progress for three reasons:

- They experience valuation problems or, in other words, they are worried about choosing the wrong option.

- They feel they lack information and are concerned that they haven't done enough homework.

- They have outcome uncertainty or fear they won't get what they're paying for.

We will cover in more detail how technical experts can partner with salespeople to reduce these percentages and help (prospective) customers move to customer improvement opportunities more effectively and more quickly.

3

Debunking Myths That Prevent Technical Experts From Driving Growth And Loyalty

W ithout a background in sales best practices and buying research, technical experts will have to rely on their own assumptions of what it takes to impact customer growth and loyalty. Although some of these assumptions will probably make logical sense, they are less likely to lead to client growth *and* retention. Instead, they can lead to inefficiencies in the end-to-end sales and delivery processes and potentially reduce a company's credibility and impact.

In this chapter I will cover two assumptions that most technical experts make and discuss why holding on to these beliefs will reduce the commercial impact throughout the end-to-end sales and delivery approach.

Myth 1: Great product and delivery service leads to account growth

In 2019 Gartner surveyed over 750 B2B customer stakeholders across twenty-four industries. The survey found that, at the time, the vast majority (88%) of account managers believed that providing above-and-beyond customer service was the surest way to drive growth.[25]

This belief is also held by people in many other roles (including technical experts) and in the research I conducted, 88.6% agree with the statement.

Based on this belief, account managers use different approaches to stimulate retention and growth. They seem to prefer to operate in a linear sequence. First they want to deliver on the commitments made with the customer, second they will ensure there is product and service consumption. These two approaches lay the foundation for the third approach: exceeding customer expectations. All three of these approaches will help to retain the business of the customer, but what about growth? Once the account manager is exceeding customer expectations, they feel they can move across the 'permission threshold' to sell additional services and expand the relationship.

However, raising the degree of service rarely helps account managers to move across the permission threshold into growth territory. The ROI on raising service levels is not lineair; beyond a certain level of service, the positive effects of this approach start decreasing and eventually disappear. Unfortunately, this happens before account managers can reach the point where they can stimulate growth. Additional efforts committed to raising the level of service become wasted efforts. Put simply, providing better service can improve customer retention, but its positive effects vanish before customer growth can be reached.[26]

This common assumption puts pressure on internal people and technical experts who help sell and service the account. It leads to offering free products (or product features) and services or getting technical experts to deliver advice which would otherwise be paid for. Some of you may be familiar with the sentence: 'Could we please offer this for free? We detect a lot of potential for additional business with this account...'

The Gartner research shows that while high levels of customer service do, in fact, increase the likelihood of customer retention, they have no statistical nor meaningful impact on growth. This means that if a salesperson over-services, they will not necessarily sell more or different services and products. What is earned is the right to keep the current business. The only way to secure growth is to consistently focus on customer improvement activities because those drive both client retention and growth.

In the research, customer improvement activities were defined as:

- Helping to create ROI of commercial partnership

- Educating the client on potential risks they may face when pursuing a specific course of action

- Helping to drive business outcomes

To achieve these outcomes throughout the end-to-end sales and delivery process, salespeople need to partner and align with technical experts. The goal needs to be to link salespeople's input and technical expertise to customer expectations, as we will discuss later in this chapter.

Myth 2: Strong client relationships lead to new business and growth

Within a sales organisation, one in five salespeople on average is a 'relationship builder'. This is one of the five typical sales profiles the Challenger research identified.[27] As the name suggests, relationship builders nurture strong personal and professional relationships. They are generous with their time and will work hard to ensure the customers get what they need. Celebrating the end of a project, or an extension on an existing or new contract, is a good reason to organise a nice lunch or dinner and proof of a strong client relationship.

In an economic downturn, all costs are under scrutiny, including the cost of sales. Add the COVID-19 restrictions, which made it harder to meet people in person, and it becomes clear that classic relationship builders will be feeling uncomfortable. They are cornered and forced to rethink their relationship strategies. Before COVID-19, it took an average of six face-to-face business trips or meetings to close a large deal. Now they have to achieve the same outcome in only three.[28] Not all industries are equally affected, but new context changes have forced everyone to think differently on how to engage and how to maximise the time with and impact on customers, using different media and digital communication channels.

The Challenger sales research was conducted using an extensive evidence-based approach and has already proven that when it comes to selling in a complex B2B environment, the classic relationship-building approach is a losing approach. In a more complex B2B sales environment, the Challenger profile is 4.5 times more likely to be a high performer than any other profile. Challenger profiles will also achieve, on average, 13% higher goal attainment than other sales profiles.[29]

	Transactional	Complex
Relationship builder	11%	4%
Problem solver	18%	7%
Hard worker	26%	10%
Lone wolf	25%	25%
Challenger	20%	54%

Percentage of high performance by sales profile in low-and high complexity B2B sales environments from CEB Sales Executive Council Research, as cited in The Challenger Sale, 2011. © *Challenger Performance Optimization, Inc*

Why is being a relationship builder a losing approach in a complex B2B sales environment? Because a high number of customer stakeholders is needed to close any given sale, and it is almost impossible to build this type of relationship with so many people. On top of that, we see a lot more movement in stakeholders across businesses, which means someone else may have to pick up a discussion on an opportunity from scratch in a long sales cycle.

The true believers in this type of relationship building often assume that there is only one way to build relationships successfully, but there is no universal professional relationship-building approach. A good analogy is to consider how bartenders build professional relationships with their customers versus how personal fitness trainers build professional relationships with their clients. What characterises both types of relationships?

A bartender takes an order. They lend a sympathetic ear and agree with the customer. A personal fitness trainer builds successful client relationships by stretching their client's thinking, challenging the client, building a case for changing behaviours by tailoring the communication and approach, and pushing the client to work harder to help them achieve better health outcomes. It is a case of providing comfort versus challenge.

Building a professional relationship entirely on agreeing with the client's current approach and never respectfully challenging them means a salesperson may temporarily retain their current business but is unlikely to be consulted for advice on how to do things differently. To obtain loyalty or growth, it is necessary to redefine views on professional relationships and to put longer-term customer improvements at the heart of the approach. Customer improvement activities and behaviours should be the core of a professional relationship.

New opportunities to impact client loyalty and growth

As we have seen, many people are currently affected by these two assumptions, which makes it unlikely that the role of technical expert is being used effectively to positively impact loyalty and growth outcomes. By continuing to hold on to these false beliefs, technical experts will focus on the wrong actions and activities (eg over-servicing on projects, delivering project work at lower margins and agreeing to every customer request to avoid damaging the client relationship).

Given that the buying process is neither linear nor predictable, we need to offer everyone who can impact the end-to-end sales and delivery process a better understanding of which key buyer expectations can drive towards growth and loyalty.

In this section, I will review critical buyer expectations which, if fulfilled by different people in different roles, can lead to a positive purchasing experience. I will also share how technical experts can play a unique role in fulfilling or exceeding these expectations. Having a greater understanding of critical buyer expectations will empower technical experts to maximise commercial opportunities at any moment and prepare for interactions with customer stakeholders.

When I asked the respondents in my research about whether they believe they can contribute to a great purchase experience, 74% said they believe they can.

Technical experts and stakeholders working in expert delivery teams, order processing and pre- and post-sales service teams etc need to be treated as commercial extensions of the sales force. They should get to play more than just a mechanical and technical role in the process. If commercially aligned to customer expectations, the sum of the efforts of all the individual players will contribute greatly to creating a positive purchase experience. Let's consider each of the customer expectations that can impact growth and client retention in more detail and how they present as opportunities for technical experts to play a role in aligning to these expectations.[30]

Offers unique and valuable perspectives on the market

A strong commercial teaching message or customer improvement insight should aim to solve a business challenge and explain how a (prospective) customer can take advantage of a business opportunity and lead towards a solution. Although several sales methodologies aim to lead clients to new solutions, the key to creating a successful customer improvement insight message is thorough preparation and a strong understanding of the economic and customer value drivers.

Salespeople are not the only employees who can offer unique customer improvement insights and valuable perspectives on the market. Anyone supporting interactions with customers can offer an individual perspective and teach something new which could trigger customer change.

Customers are also most likely to reset their buying criteria when they are confronted with surprising information about their business. Strong commercial teaching messages can be created in partnership with technical experts who have different perspectives on the market context, stakeholder assumptions and their personal and business needs.

The obvious partnerships between sales and marketing can lead to great messaging ideas and approaches. Multidisciplinary teams will be even more productive and valuable. Experts with different technical perspectives, such as product experts, scientists, implementation specialists, legal and technology officers, may come up with innovative ideas that no sales team could have thought up by themselves.

Differences among team members also force each member to consider and evaluate alternative and unexpected viewpoints. Reaching consensus will take more effort and people must work harder to communicate their thinking, broaden their views and consider a variety of perspectives. This takes more preparation, but it is valuable. When members of diverse teams see things in a variety of ways, they are poised to recognise new and different market opportunities and they can get a better understanding of unmet client needs. A broader partnership between different technical experts helps businesses benefit from the value of diversity of thought.[31] Those experts are also more likely to thoroughly consider what questions and objections may surface in the buying groups.

Technical experts often take pride in applying their knowledge and may see the challenge of constantly being on the lookout for new advice and business opportunities as a new intellectual problem to solve.

Earlier we looked at buying analysis paralysis. Too much information and too many options also presents an opportunity for technical experts to collaborate directly or indirectly with people in a buyer organisation. They can help consolidate and influence potential buying from stakeholders, using different media and channels to pinpoint the type of business problems organisations are not able to see clearly.

Helps the buyer navigate alternatives and provides ongoing advice or consultation

Buyers need to stay relevant if they want to keep up with today's fast-paced and changing world of work. They have an opportunity to adopt new approaches and navigate potential obstacles to keep their core activities running or to come up with new ways to service a new market demand. It is critical that they continue to learn to understand all possible alternatives before going in a new direction, embarking on an important project or implementing a solution. Buyers need to be confident that there is consensus within their organisation that a business problem is worth solving before moving towards a solution.

There is a vast amount of reliable, high-quality and trustworthy information out there, but for more complex solutions the available information can be difficult to process. Sometimes the messages are even conflicting. According to Gartner research from 2019, the average buying group spends 15% of the buying cycle time reconciling and prioritising that conflicting information.[32] In the early stages, the buying process can stall because there are too many diverging views which cannot be reconciled. When nobody is able to facilitate a consensus, the business problem will remain unaddressed and the formal pursuit of a supplier with a solution is put on the backburner.

B2B buyers expect suppliers to support open, connected, intuitive and immediate exchanges that enable the buying group as they move through their buying decision process.[33] There will probably be a more important role for more advanced technology integration and artificial intelligence in facilitating buyer support in the future. This could help to offer contextual and relevant information and to answer questions as they surface. When purchasing a solution in a complex B2B world, however, it is likely that buyer questions will be unique or linked to a specific context or challenge. A relevant answer or piece of advice surfaces after applying the right doses of unique human skills, such as critical thinking, innovation, collaboration, change management and, especially, the ability to provide the answer in a compelling way, which we will look at later in the book.[34] Skills such as connecting different pieces of information or tailoring advice to a variety of stakeholders will not be replaced by buyer support technology any time soon.

Technical experts with an understanding of the broader commercial context within an organisation are well placed to facilitate learning in buyer groups. If well prepared, they can play a role in anticipating potential stakeholder questions, hurdles and objections which may otherwise stop the buyers from making a decision.

Technical experts can also play a key role in sharing their experiences from sales and delivery interactions with other colleagues to effectively turn these pieces of information into best practice guidance. This can be used as advice for other potential buyers. Their advice is more likely to be trusted if there is no immediate sale on the horizon. Organisations who get ongoing consultation and trustworthy advice from a diverse set of stakeholders will see this as another contributor to a great commercial experience, and this can eventually be rewarded with loyalty and growth.

Educates on new outcomes and potential risks

Stakeholders within a buying or client organisation can be stuck in their mental models or habits, preventing them from seeing different and new potential outcomes. They can also be wrong about their problem, not seeing all its causes or not being able to articulate the problem well. Incorrect assumptions or choices made in the buying process could lead to a problematic delivery of the solutions. 'Bartender' type relationship builders may find it daunting to go against the client's views. They prefer to agree with the client's request in the hope that this strengthens the relationship.

Buyers may have a power advantage because they can agree or disagree on a purchase, but they don't have the same experience as a supplier who can refer to their knowledge of numerous client scenarios and implementation experiences. Technical experts should respectfully challenge clients if they anticipate potential risks, even if the risks are not directly tied to the product or solution itself.

REFLECTION: CUSTOMISATION REQUESTS

Almost every client will review products and solutions from a perspective of customisation flexibility. This can be triggered by a genuine business need; however, in most instances it relies on the perception that they are different. Probing for the relevance and/or sharing the potential risks or consequences of customisation requests is not standard behaviour. The customer is king, so these requests get passed on to technical delivery teams and don't always get challenged. It can, however, be the type of challenge clients will appreciate because it helps them avoid risk. The picture below shows an example of a customisation trade-off triangle, which I have used to challenge customisation requests.

Client specific need

Customisation
trade-off triangle

Implementation ease
(time, cost, quality,...)

Proven customer
improvement outcomes

The customisation trade-off triangle

If a client asks for new customisation to a solution, it is likely this will impact the implementation and the proven outcomes. What is more important? Does the client understand that every customisation decision may have some potential risks or trade-offs?

Technical experts can work with salespeople to come up with information to demonstrate the impact of this triangle on key solutions and products. The experience of most technical experts is then reused whenever these questions surface. If done well, this information can be applied to different client situations and/or enabling new joiners in sales and delivery teams.

For this approach to be successful, it requires people who can collaborate across teams and silos and see different perspectives. However, to have a longer-lasting impact, a more structural partnership between sales and experienced technical experts is required to bring together their invaluable collective knowledge and experience (for example, by populating the customisation trade-off triangle). Customers will then get in-depth advice on the key products and solutions they want to buy, which is worth a lot more than a glossy product or services brochure.

Gives buyers the means to get widespread support

Most roles in a supplier organisation can have a direct or indirect impact on the buying experience of its potential customers. Whether you work in a legal, product, implementation or finance role, it is worthwhile reviewing where and how you can positively impact the buyer experience from your own role and perspective. What can you do to simplify information or educate buyers in a proactive way? Which parts of the broader end-to-end sales and delivery processes create a common delay, a hurdle or frustration for internal and external stakeholders?

According to research from Gartner in 2019, customers who feel the information they receive from suppliers helps advance their buying tasks are 2.8 times more likely to experience a high degree of purchase ease, and 3 times more likely to buy a bigger deal with less regret.[35]

REFLECTION: BUYER ENABLEMENT

In a company I worked for, the terms and conditions of the contracts always included an important standard clause to protect the intellectual property of the organisation. This clause always caused a delay in contract negotiations because every large buying organisation puts their own clause in contracts, stating something along the lines of 'Everything delivered by a supplier to the buying organisation becomes intellectual property of the buying organisation.' Requesting to remove this clause to protect our organisation's intellectual property was an ongoing battle and became a hurdle to driving contracts to successful closure. Frustrations from sales as well as the technical buyers were often difficult to manage. Our commercially focused legal team created a great example of a buyer enablement support tool. They had written a simple and short educational flyer outlining why it was critical to keep some terms and conditions in our contracts. Rather than this being an objection that each sales representative needed to deal with individually as a reaction to a concern from the customer's legal experts, this short summary became an educational tool to proactively share with the stakeholders of the buyer organisation.

PART TWO

COSMOS: A COMMERCIAL FRAMEWORK FOR TECHNICAL EXPERTS

In Part Two I will discuss COSMOS, a commercial framework that I have devised which provides a structure for technical experts to increase their commercial impact and empowers them to take ownership of their commercial capability development. It is easy to get started with the framework, and it doesn't take months to implement. It offers a detailed roadmap with specific considerations for technical experts to prepare for customer improvement in most commercial situations. It focuses on *what* to prepare for to reach commercial impact in the most effective way.

The word COSMOS refers to an 'orderly or harmonious entity'. As a commercial framework, it offers a simple and pragmatic structure to make sense of what can be perceived as a chaotic sales universe, which has little to do with the day-to-day world of technical experts. COSMOS stands for:

- Context: What's happening in the world of the customer?

- Opportunities: Which opportunities can drive customer improvement?

- Stakeholders: Who will (not) care about customer improvement?

- Motivation: What motivates (no) change?

- Obstacles (or Objections): Which obstacles can hinder the journey towards change?

- Strategy: What's your plan to realise new commercial outcomes?

Under each of these key topics, I will outline the relevant areas to prepare for to maximise commercial contributions. The framework will help focus on the most relevant information that needs to be prepared to impact customer improvement. It is designed to empower technical experts to ask the relevant questions to salespeople when working together on commercial opportunities. Every individual can take full ownership to raise the bar on how they impact customer outcomes and improve their commercial understanding.

4

Context: What's Happening In The World Of The Customer?

Many organisations do not expect commercial capabilities of or contributions from people outside the sales department, but commercial capabilities are going to become critical for many people in the future workforce, not just for salespeople and leaders. Making a commercial contribution does not mean being responsible for a revenue number. In a complex B2B sales context, focusing on customer improvement activities can also drive client retention and growth. It is more likely to appeal to technical experts than the prospect of having to sell something or achieving a sales number.

Customer improvement activities were defined by Gartner in 2019 as the articulation of an ROI on the commercial partnership between the supplier and the customer, the education of the customer on potential risks they may face when pursuing a specific course of action, and sharing a vision towards improved business outcomes.[36] Buyers also expect suppliers to be easy to work with and have widespread buy-in in their organisation.[37] This creates a long list of opportunities for technical experts to help drive commercial impact.

Technical experts may never see any formal mention in their job description or goals that relates to these specific customer improvement activities. Clarifying these new future workforce expectations could be a good starting point to make all employees more accountable for making an impact and initiating customer improvement activities.

Achieving customer improvement

To increase your commercial awareness and/or capability, it is important to learn more about the context of the customers you can potentially impact. Thinking critically about the customer's business can seem overwhelming, but there is no need to have a detailed understanding of everything that is required to be successful in a specific organisation or to acquire specific industry knowledge. To increase your commercial contributions, there is only one foundational principle to uphold: to demonstrate curiosity outside of your own technical domain and to learn a few key things about the customer and the larger external environment they operate in.

There are three questions you need to answer to understand how you can potentially help achieve customer improvement.

1. What are the key changes happening in the industry?

Having a good understanding of the world of the customer does not mean you need to be an industry expert. You do, however, need to understand the bigger topics at play in the industry, for example, important technological shifts, new government regulations, strategic moves by competitors, sustainability initiatives or key mergers and acquisitions.

These types of important changes are likely to be picked up by business news media and published on external websites. There are additional sources you can consult for interesting industry news: industry trade groups, industry papers or even analyst reports.

Having a broader understanding of what is going on with the customer and within their industry, and then coupling this with your technical expertise, may allow new insights on possible customer improvement opportunities to surface. As an expert in your domain and someone with an external perspective, you can most likely connect different pieces of information together in a new way, which could translate into an insight or a new opportunity on how a customer can improve their business.

Every organisation operates in a broader industry context, which brings us to our second question.

2. How does the organisation make money?

Can you identify the most important revenue streams for the organisation? Revenue can be defined as the amount of money a company receives from its customers in exchange for the sales of goods or services. Sometimes a company's revenue stream may not be immediately obvious. As an example, the fast-food chain McDonalds moved into real estate and found a new creative revenue stream by using their pre-existing capital. A new revenue opportunity can arise from looking at what's available, connecting different sources of information and thinking critically (and out of the box) about new commercial possibilities.

Revenue is the top-line item on an income statement from which all costs and expenses are subtracted to arrive at net income. A bit of (manageable) research on the company will help you find the answer to this question.

3. What are the organisational goals to improve business performance?

Every organisation has a reason to exist, a key purpose or mission. Organisations fulfil this purpose and organise resources in a way to be best positioned **to drive**

growth in a healthy and sustainable way. Let's look more closely at the concepts 'growth' and 'health'.

Organisations can grow by gaining access to new markets through successful mergers and acquisitions or by opening new locations. In these instances, they apply what is called an **inorganic** growth strategy. If organisations choose to grow **organically**, they mainly focus on creating financial health (eg sufficient cash, revenue, profits or healthy margins and costs) and people health (eg a great employee experience, engagement and wellbeing) within their organisation. The importance of realising positive people health outcomes has increased because individuals' wellbeing, productivity and prosperity are at the core of all successful economies and firms.[38]

In the new world of work, additional areas of measurement to quantify the value of human capital within an organisation are going to become more important than in previous decades. Without people health, new commercial opportunities and innovation are less likely to happen. Organisations with a focus on wellbeing, a great employee experience and engagement obtain better company and customer results. Productivity can be maintained or improved but it can come at a price. Research from surveys conducted before and during the pandemic, drawing on data from more than 20,000 employees, revealed that COVID-19 has negatively impacted the workforce health of 55% of the global workforce.[39] According to Gartner in 2021, in surveys taken before and after the pandemic, work-force health was measured across three main factors – healthy employees, healthy relationships and healthy work environments – and the survey looked at multiple workforce wellbeing elements, including work–life balance, psychological safety, burnout, collaboration, innovation and responsiveness.[40]

An organisation also needs financial health to be able to invest in assets such as products, operations and people, to create new opportunities or to better align to changing market needs. Both financial and people health are critical and can't exist without each other – at least not for a sustainable longer period. The art is to find the right balance of the different drivers to achieve sustainable growth and business performance.

CEOs set organisational goals, or priorities, to align internal teams in the pursuit of greater business performance. These goals usually have a relatively stable time horizon and are communicated at least once a year to employees and more regularly to investors (for example, on earnings calls if the company is publicly listed).

Organisational goals to impact business growth in a healthy and sustainable way can come in many flavours, but if you look at them more carefully you can narrow them down to three types. **Increasing efficiency** covers all initiatives under the umbrella 'doing more with less'. **Transforming the organisation** focuses on finding a new purpose or either adding new or enhancing existing capabilities to better align to different market, organisational or people needs. **Reducing risks** applies to human, system or process errors.

These three types of organisational goals are not mutually exclusive: a CEO can simultaneously set more than one type of goal for the organisation to focus on. Of course, some departments can have a bigger share and impact on achieving a specific organisational goal. In essence, these goals are foundational pillars to help steer initiatives towards growth in company performance.

To identify customer improvement opportunities, it is important to understand the higher-level organisational goals and business challenges a company is facing.

The first component of the COSMOS framework focuses on what to prepare for to better understand the customer's context. Before we move on to the second, it is helpful to ask yourself the following questions: What did I learn? Which connections can I make that could help the customer do business in a better way? How can my expertise or solution (products and/or services) potentially help to address (new) customer issues?

5

Opportunities: Which Opportunities Can Drive Customer Improvement?

The second section of the COSMOS framework helps you reflect on what type of customer improvement opportunities you can explore to help the customer build a better business. The following questions will help you formulate your ideas:

- **Can you fulfil one or more key buyer expectations leading to retention and growth?**

  Are you able to offer a unique and valuable perspective on the market the customer operates in? Can you help navigate alternatives and provide ongoing advice or consultation? Will you educate on new outcomes and potential risks? How will you make it easy to buy from your organisation and create additional buy-in for your organisation as a supplier?

- **Can you link the (underappreciated) capabilities of your solution to a specific customer challenge or pain point?**

  Think about challenges or pain points that the organisation may be facing. Are you able to connect your unique expertise or the capabilities of your solution to key desired client outcomes?

- **Is there a way to achieve a high(er) level of return or customer impact?**

  Suppliers can have three types of impact on the customer with their solutions (products and/or services):

  Level 1 – Proven organisational outcomes

  Level 2 – Perceived business impact

  Level 3 – Solution (feature) satisfaction

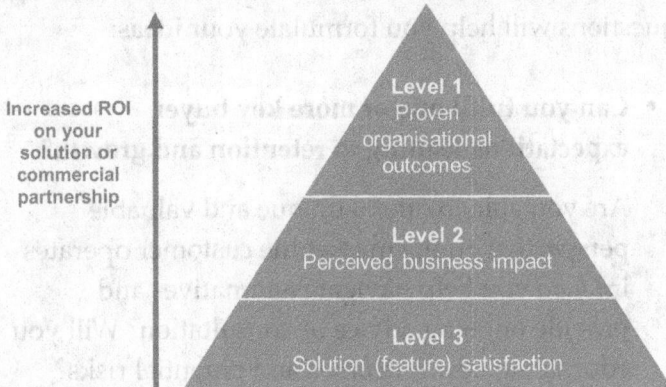

Increased ROI on your solution or commercial partnership

Level 1
Proven organisational outcomes

Level 2
Perceived business impact

Level 3
Solution (feature) satisfaction

The type of impact of commercial partnerships

The most desirable level of impact (for suppliers and customers) occurs when the link between your company's product or solution and the customer's organisational performance outcomes (eg reduced costs, increased revenues or increased customer loyalty) can be clearly proven. This relationship helps to demonstrate the ROI of the solution or product and, as a result, the commercial partnership the customer has with your organisation. It is, however, not always easy to make a direct link between complex solutions and tangible organisational performance outcomes.

The second level of impact connects your solution to solving (part of) a business challenge and achieving a positive business outcome. Is a given department seeing an increase in activity or impact in a specific area? The relationship may not be statistically proven, but it is clear the implementation of your solution has made a difference.

The majority of commercial partnerships will get stuck at level three: solution (feature) satisfaction. This implies that the solution is not clearly linked to organisational performance outcomes or impacting a business challenge. The customer is, however, satisfied with the solution or specific features of the solution (eg training, data dashboards, implementation, consulting services, project management, customer service support, software or technology enhancements).

A commercial partnership which is only based on a level three type impact may be scrutinised when costs need to be cut. In fact, most commercial partnerships have difficulties renewing if there is no clear articulation on customer improvement impact. Especially in a period of budget constraints, there should be urgency within a supplier organisation to review and articulate how to move the impact of a solution from just 'satisfaction' to 'perceived business impact' or, even better, to 'proven impact on organisational performance'. Salespeople and technical experts can review on a regular basis how this can be established in a proactive way rather than wait until it is too late.

Formalising a customer improvement opportunity

A customer improvement opportunity can be written using the three ingredients in the order listed below:

- ◎ **Organisational growth goal**: Name the most obvious organisational objective you are likely impacting (eg increasing efficiency, transforming the organisation and reducing risk).

- ⋏ **Business challenge**: Name the business challenge you believe you can solve.

- ✕ **Your solution**: Briefly describe how your expertise and your products and services help solve the challenge by focusing on one or more key business levers, such as people, processes and tools.

There are a few important considerations to keep in mind when you craft your customer improvement statement. It should:

- Always start with the customer

- Share a hypothesis based on your understanding of the world of the customer's context and their objectives

- Be specific and aligned to a clear organisational objective

- Use customer language

- Be jargon-free and concise so that it can be easily retold to other people whom you did not speak to directly

---

REFLECTION: A MESSAGE THAT CAN BE UNDERSTOOD BY ALL

Crafting a good customer improvement statement gets easier with practice. From my experience in training technical experts and salespeople on the topic of customer improvement (also called 'business value articulation'), I found that on average it takes someone less than an hour to come up with a clear customer improvement statement for the first time.

The art is to create a message which can be understood by someone who doesn't work in your domain; the message should have a 'retell-ability' factor. This can only happen if the neutral listener can give you feedback on whether it is clear what customer outcome you are trying to achieve, what business challenge you are tackling and how you can help the customer improve their business with your solution, products or services. This shows you think 'customer first'.

Your message should be simple and without technical jargon. Here is an example:

We help to:

◎ Reduce risk.

⋀⋀ We do this by predicting where staff turnover is most likely to happen in the organisation.

✕ Our Employee Experience Management System helps to understand the predictive drivers of flight risk and offers personalised insight and advice in a scalable way to individuals and managers in the organisation to improve this situation.

Once you have crafted your hypothesis, you should try validating your understanding with someone who knows the customer well and who may have already aligned your chosen solutions to the customer's organisational objectives and their preferred language. In any case, two perspectives probably make for a sharper and more impactful statement than one.

6

Stakeholders: Who Will (Not) Care About This Customer Improvement Opportunity?

Once you have identified a customer improvement opportunity, the next key element in the COSMOS framework is to work out who may be influencing and/or deciding on potential change by finding out which key stakeholders you are most likely impacting with your solution and what these people are focused on. The adoption of a new complex solution in an organisation is unlikely to happen when only one stakeholder is convinced of the need to do so. Most businesses exist in a risk-averse context, and it is unlikely that people will want to attach their name to a solution implementation that may potentially fail. The fear of messing up is a major cause for not agreeing on going for a new solution and why 40% to 60% of commercial opportunities never go anywhere.[41] Adopting complex solutions in today's B2B buying context typically involves a group of six to ten people who need to reach a consensus on a shared cause or challenge that everyone wants to solve.

Depending on the type of customer improvement you need, first try to understand who should at least care about this improvement because doing so is part of their role and expected outcomes – although on its own this is not enough. We know that human beings are not purely logical. There may be several reasons why someone does not want to change the status quo.

In this chapter we will look at how you can avoid the key issues with stakeholder management: not knowing who the key stakeholders are, investing too much time with the wrong people and not spending enough time with the right stakeholders.

Uniting the right stakeholders

Functional leaders (or department heads) translate organisational goals into their own objectives. Every functional team is on point to align with and execute on these priorities, using their own resources and tackling the business challenges with relevant tools, processes and people.

To illustrate this, I have chosen three roles that are often involved in the buying process of complex B2B solutions: a chief revenue (or sales) officer, a head of procurement and a chief operations officer. In the table below, you will see examples of their respective missions, functional objectives, operational metrics and some key trends or concerns.

Every function or department (eg sales, operations, finance, legal) has its own mission, resources and objectives. Well-defined functional boundaries and objectives help everyone in the department to have a clear purpose and feel accountable to reach functional outcomes they can easily relate to. They provide a sense of control and influence in a specific part of the organisation.

Many leaders try to handle complexity around them by doubling down on what is being asked of them. They say: 'Hey, there is a lot going on out there. If we don't focus on our functional priorities, it is going to be really easy to get distracted.' In other words, many leaders have an individual focus, which means they concentrate on their individual tasks, team and functional unit. These functional silos can make consensus-buying decisions harder when buying complex solutions across different functions for the greater good of the organisation.

To reach consensus and solve a business challenge that goes beyond function and impacts overall organisational performance, you need to find stakeholders who act as 'enterprise leaders'. Enterprise leaders can look beyond their own tasks and also leverage

Different focus areas of functional stakeholders

	Stakeholder A: Chief revenue officer	Stakeholder B: Head of procurement	Stakeholder C: Chief operations officer
Mission	Generating sustainable revenue streams by driving integration and alignment between all revenue-related functions and creating a great customer experience	Creating competitive advantage by delivering greater ROI on commercial partnerships (eg by reducing risk and improving profit) and relationships with suppliers	Generating a competitive advantage through operations by aligning business objectives with the available resources
Functional objectives	• New business acquisition • Client loyalty and increased cross-selling • Expanded margins and profitability • Increased revenue and market share • Commercial enablement and development of customer-facing teams	• Rationalising suppliers • Aligning the functional goals with broader corporate strategy goals • Managing risk in the supply chain • Tracking savings and broader impact • Driving adoption of procurement processes and initiatives • Being involved early in sourcing projects	• Improving margins and profitability of the business • Implementation and tracking of continuous improvement initiatives • Translation of corporate strategy into business results

Examples	Stakeholder A: Chief revenue officer	Stakeholder B: Head of procurement	Stakeholder C: Chief operations officer
Operational metrics	• Time to productivity • Gap to revenue goals • Opportunity–win ratio • Profitability • Customer acquisition costs	• Total cost savings • ROI on cost-reduction initiatives • Supplier quality metrics • Contract compliance	• Prompt performance • Quality metrics • Improved margins • Environmental sustainability metrics
Trends and concerns	• Consensus buying • Global customers and employees • Enabling effective hybrid/remote working practices • Customers learning from non-direct supplier channels and interactions • Increased procurement and sourcing agreements • Increased margins • Developing staff to fulfil future workforce requirements	• Unplanned spending • Internal buy-in • Ensuring alignment to internal stakeholder needs • Increasing standardising and digitisation and/or digitalisation of processes and tools	• Quality risks of suppliers • Managing the shifting global demands of business and customers • Shifting focus from technical requirements to customer needs • Sharing risks with suppliers

their resources and teams for the greater organisational good. It is frightening that only 12% of leaders in organisations are effective enterprise leaders.[42] We can easily assume that it will be hard work if seven out of eight leaders are mostly looking after their own functional interests and are unwilling to lose focus and energy on something that clearly goes beyond the domain of their functional control.

If you multiply the number of perspectives in the table above by two or three, it will align more closely to a realistic buying stakeholder group. Without the help of a supplier, it is hard for these stakeholders to articulate a clear customer improvement statement or a shared cause on their own. It is in the supplier's best interest to facilitate consensus around a clear shared cause.

The key is to ask yourself what all the key customer stakeholders (at least) 'temporarily' have in common that could help to unite them. Is there a problem everyone is impacted by? If you take the three stakeholder roles mentioned above, you can tailor the benefits of your solution to only one specific stakeholder's functional priorities, which may help win one person over. An agreement is, however, more than the sum of separate 'yes' responses. Buying decisions are successful only if all stakeholders work through the decision-making process together.

Looking for 'Mobilizers®'

There are seven distinct customer profiles which exist in the context of both working with suppliers and driving change across their organisations. The summaries and the table below of this research, are published in *The Challenger Customer*.[43] Of the seven profiles, not all are equally useful, but some employees excel at rallying their organisations to act and ultimately drive consensus and change. These people have what we call **Mobilizer** profiles. Another term for a mobilizer is a 'change agent.'

Mobilizer profiles from The Challenger Customer research[44]

Mobilizer profiles	Someone with this profile is...	And you should...
The go-getter: 'Show us the business value and we will get it done.'	...focused on organisational improvement and prone to championing new ideas and their implementation.	...prioritise organisational benefit, provide a clear vision and ensure they can convey this vision.
The teacher: 'I love this idea! Let's save the details for later.'	...effective at rallying others to action but weak on process management.	...stick with their vision and tweak only as needed. Provide a clear plan and timelines and keep them on track with interim milestones.

Mobilizer profiles	Someone with this profile is...	And you should...
The sceptic: 'I know how to get things done but you've got a lot to prove.'	...open to new ideas but moves cautiously after much deliberation.	...drive urgency to compel them to act. Provide absolute certainty in the project plan. Give a compelling story to share.

High-performing commercial people try to target Mobilizers in an organisation because they believe those employees can help progress their case. They avoid colleagues who willingly talk to suppliers but can't move a decision forward or have relatively little impact on organisational change. Those people are still accessible, often willing to share information and happy to talk, but relatively ineffective at convincing others to take action. As a result, these people are profiled as **talkers**.

Talker profiles from The Challenger Customer research[45]

Talker profiles	Someone with this profile is...	And you should...
The guide: 'Here is what you need to know about us...'	...willing to share information unavailable to others to demonstrate credibility and status.	...pull as much information from them as you can. Don't mistreat as a Mobilizer – they won't get things done.
The friend: 'Sure, I'll take the call – what new things can you show me?'	...receptive to supplier meetings and willing to network sales representatives with colleagues.	...not get comfortable with them – they can become a red herring and a time sink.

Talker profiles	Someone with this profile is...	And you should...
The climber: 'What's in it for me?'	...focused largely on personal advancements irrespective of organisational success.	...focus on a personal win if you think you need them. Be careful – their help can backfire if you become linked with a distrusted contact's personal agenda.

Lastly, there are **blockers**. These individuals are rarely of any help to a supplier, as they view improvement projects as a distraction and therefore will not share useful information. Blockers cannot be ignored, because they can reduce the likelihood of a high-quality deal by 47%.[46] The sooner these are identified, the better, as this will help focus time on different messaging and engagement strategies and concentrate on approaches to help minimise their impact and influence in the buying group. You cannot assume they fall into a specific functional or buying role or pattern of seniority. We will cover how to deal with blockers in Chapter 12.

Every customer has a primary profile, but they can also have traits of other customer profiles.

When you leave a meeting, a good test to see whether there is commitment to and engagement with your customer improvement idea is to provide at least one action for the customer to take on. As an example, the customer can commit to a next step such as sharing a complete list of stakeholders who may be involved in the purchase.

REFLECTION: DON'T BE FOOLED BY TITLES OR RANKS

A young graduate who was doing an internship in a well-respected international organisation called a company I worked for to inquire about our products and services. Even though he was a temporary graduate looking to learn, he was also a clear change agent and convinced about the greater good for the company. He prepared every argument to make his case for change and mobilised different internal stakeholders on his own. Not much later, he was able to orchestrate change and overhaul an established global talent process which had been there for many years to a new and more effective one.

Highly performing commercial people tend to look for Mobilizers in the organisation so that these people can get 'the village' to agree to buy their solution and create consensus.[47] As discussed earlier, technical experts can have existing relationships or dealings with different stakeholders in the buying organisation. They have a great opportunity to share their knowledge and help bring the Mobilizers to the surface and neutralise blockers for existing and new commercial opportunities.

7

Motivation: What Motivates Change Or No Change?

A long with the stakeholders comes the fourth section of the COSMOS framework: motivators. They are the elements that trigger stakeholders to change (or not).

Human beings are creatures of habit. Changing our behaviour is always hard, but it becomes even harder if the adoption of a new solution means that well-established routines and approaches have to be overhauled. In the previous section, we saw how individuals in identical roles with exactly the same goals may (or may not) be motivated to change. As an example, someone in a new role may be looking to make a quick impact and may be open to trying a new solution. A different individual in the same role who has been extensively involved in establishing the existing processes and routines may be less inclined to rock the boat.

Providing a clear ROI on a solution or a commercial partnership is expected from suppliers. It gives buyers confidence that they made the right supplier decision. It is also one of the key customer improvement activities that can lead to growth and retention – but people do not buy or renew contracts purely on rational arguments. Even if you articulate a clear customer improvement opportunity which shows that there is potential value to be gained by the customer, stakeholders can still decide not to change the situation.

REFLECTION: RESISTING OLD HABITS

Think of it this way: is your energy contract at home the best deal you can get? Why have you not yet scanned the market and changed to a different energy provider who offers better value for money? After all, this is an essential component of your household budget. The same goes for healthy living and healthy eating habits. Rationally, you know eating less sugar is the right thing to do, but when the next chocolate bar presents itself, you give in. Now imagine what it is like to move towards a change that involves adopting a new complex solution that impacts the behaviour of dozens (or even hundreds) of employees after this was agreed upon by the buying group...

If a customer improvement opportunity is clear, then the longer the customer waits to adopt it, the more they are at the mercy of the cost of staying in the current approach. These are the opportunity costs of doing nothing or doing things differently. How can you get the customer to move forward faster and build the case for stakeholders to reach a consensus decision more effectively, thus meeting the organisational objectives?

Intrinsic and extrinsic motivation

A common traditional approach is to paint a picture of a new, bright future and the journey towards this better business outcome. A more effective approach focuses on understanding what motivates the (prospective) customer to stay in the current approach. What are the underlying assumptions and beliefs that form the basis for a chosen way of dealing with a particular challenge? What is it that the customer is missing or underappreciating? People do not come to work to deliberately make ineffective business decisions or create unnecessary costs. What is going on?

The preparation you have done so far brings you to the next piece of the puzzle: a person's mental model (behaviours and beliefs), which leads to their choice of approach to achieving outcomes in the role. What will motivate the customer to move from the current to a desired new state?

Given the large number of stakeholders involved in complex B2B buying decisions, doing this preparation for a Mobilizer will yield more results than doing the same preparation for a talker. If a change agent or Mobilzer is convinced about a (new) business need which requires a change in approach, then they will be compelled to independently motivate others within their organisation.

Individuals can choose to change behaviours because they have motivation from within (**intrinsic motivation**) or a clear reason for change which is not linked to any reward or outside gain (eg personal development, wellbeing or simply the satisfaction of embarking on a new journey).

Motivation can also come from outside (**extrinsic motivation**). This is when change leads to some kind of reward or outcome (eg a promotion, status, more power or external public recognition).

You can decide to raise your commercial capabilities because your company will pay you a bonus (extrinsic motivation) or because it helps your development and keeps you interested in your job (intrinsic motivation).

The most common mistakes are giving monetary reward too much weight, projecting your own motivational drivers onto your audience or thinking that just the logic of moving towards a new, bright future will compel people to change towards it. Prompting people to change to a new state doesn't happen by spending more time articulating the benefits of this desired state but by better articulating the **pain** of staying in the current state.

Instead of explaining that your solution helps to reduce sales staff turnover, you need to paint a picture of staff reduction in real human terms. For instance: 'Right now one in six people walking into the building is either considering leaving or actively making plans to move to a role at another company. What if you have to send the resignation announcement about the best person in your team? Who can you afford to see leave? What's the impact on the morale in the team if the additional person who leaves is carrying the missing revenue target needed for a bonus pay-out?'

These human consequences of staff turnover will trigger different intrinsic and/or extrinsic motivators. The pain of staying in the current state should also be bigger than the pain of change if we want the stakeholder to move to the desired state.

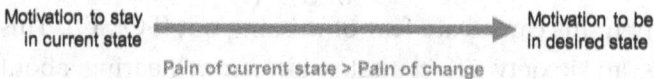

Motivation to stay ————————————————▶ Motivation to be
in current state   in desired state

Pain of current state > Pain of change

Understanding the value of change

Mobilizers are more likely to champion change for the benefit of the organisation, rather than doing this for their personal benefit. The latter is behaviour you can expect from talkers.[48] Agreeing on a buying decision is not easy, because many conflicting stakeholder perspectives need to be deconflicted. If a Mobilizer has an intrinsic motivator to drive change and move things along, then they are more likely to be resilient to the challenges and frustrations which can arise from B2B buying processes.

The influence of social media

A lot of stakeholders share valuable information on their preferences and motivators publicly; for example, on social media or at professional networking events. They share how proud they are of specific projects or ideas. This information can help you to create a hypothesis of topics that matter to the stakeholders and could be indicative of their motivation to change (or not).

In some instances, stakeholders will move towards a new approach because change is happening among colleagues who are considered to be industry leaders or influencers. If the change gets publicly broadcasted, then this can create fear of missing out (FOMO). This is an anxiety effect that arises from hearing about events happening elsewhere and feeling left behind.

The need to understand people's motivation to influence change is not something that applies only in the context of winning stakeholders over to new customer improvement opportunities – it is core to change management in general.

Technical experts who work mostly behind the front-line salespeople can see opportunities to move customers to a new recommendation or approach in a project or solution implementation. This requires them to seek to understand why people are where they are and to facilitate change, effectively *beating the status quo situation* by describing the pain of the current state and not focusing just on rational arguments.

More recent research has shown that you can't increase FOMO too much; at a certain point it can turn into fear of messing up and not moving forward at all.[49] Successful salespeople and technical experts need to know how to *sell change* and *overcome the indecision*.

In Chapter 2, I summarised some relevant findings of the Jolt research, which looked at three reasons (prospective) clients are indecisive to progress.[50] Thinking of ways we can remove obstacles (or objections) which can hinder the journey of buying a new solution leads nicely into our next part of the COSMOS framework.

8

Obstacles (Or Objections): Which Obstacles Can Hinder The Journey Towards Change?

The fifth section of the COSMOS model looks at obstacles and the role they play in the process that can lead to a buying decision or to buying indecision. Reaching a consensus decision on a new purchase is difficult and so is the process of change towards adopting a new approach or solution. Everyone working with a potential customer needs to therefore make sure that the path to the desired state is seamless so that people feel reassured that they won't mess up. If there are potential obstacles to be expected on this path, then these shouldn't come as a surprise to anyone. Most people do not like surprises. Anticipating which hurdles could be in the way of reaching buyer consensus, or on the path to the new desired state, is therefore a critical piece of analysis we need to prepare to drive change and commercial impact.

Technical experts usually gain valuable perspectives and experiences from dealing with many customers in selling and delivering solutions. They are often best placed to share their learnings directly or indirectly with the customer stakeholder group. Sales and technical experts have an opportunity to work together to anticipate potential stakeholder questions and objections which may paralyse the buyers when making a decision to change. It is important that the information provided by suppliers is neutral and easy to consume for a change agent who wants to share it within the buyer group and help create consensus within their organisation.

It may seem counterintuitive to identify objections or obstacles proactively with a potential buyer. Why would you bring something up about your solution which could potentially derail the process or plant a seed of doubt in the mind of the customer? There are, however, benefits to this process.

Objections present opportunities

Successful commercial people are not afraid of objections, because objections present opportunities. Technical experts need to take this into account as well because an objection that has been expressed explains what is going on in the mind of the customer. It is a chance to overturn false assumptions and reground them in the value of the potential customer improvement. It also creates an opportunity to fulfil buying expectations which lead to retention and growth by providing ongoing advice and educating on potential risks and different outcomes.

Customers want to know beforehand if they are going to face hurdles. If you have anticipated the obstacles in advance and offered guidance on how to deal with them, then this is likely to fulfil their critical buyer expectations.

Going back to the Mobilizer profiles: the sceptic may raise objections to be absolutely certain of the recommended plan. This doesn't mean they don't like your solution or recommendation. To sell change internally they need to have anticipated every possible obstacle or objection and have a clear approach to dealing with these. The same applies for teachers and go-getters who want to present something that is rock-solid or convey a vision and a clear path towards better organisational outcomes.

It is not because a stakeholder sees benefits in changing to a new approach that they are also willing and able to invest in fixing the problem. Finally, even if the key stakeholders agree on the benefits of fixing the problem, the organisation may decide not to use outside help. If there are enough internal resources, then they may decide not to enter a commercial relationship with an external supplier.

It is helpful at this point to reflect on your answers to two critical questions: 'Which obstacles can hinder the journey to change?' and 'Will outside help from a supplier be welcomed to solve the issue?'

9

Strategy: Where To Focus To Realise Commercial Outcomes

This section of the COSMOS framework allows you to put all your preparation to the test. To enable change towards new commercial outcomes, you need to come up with a good strategy.

Customers have myriad decisions to make and options to consider to deliver corporate goals and stay on course to achieve growth and business performance. As highlighted in previous chapters, as a technical expert there are many ways to (directly or indirectly) impact customer improvement activities, which can all lead to new commercial opportunities and greater client retention and growth.

In this section we review your customer improvement strategy from three angles, or the three Ps:

priorities, processes and (action) plan. Which opportunity should you focus on dealing with to maximise resources and impact? What are the expectations within the buyer process and in the sales and delivery process? To drive results, how will you monitor progress with a clear plan and well-thought-through actions?

Priorities: Picking low-hanging fruit or planting a new fruit tree?

If you have defined a list of customer improvement opportunities, it is worth looking at whether each opportunity helps to fulfil a customer need or creates a customer need.

Fulfilling a need

When an organisation reaches a consensus that a specific business problem needs to be addressed, then potential solution providers can be invited to participate in a formal RFP process. When this happens, the buyer group of a (prospective) customer organisation has travelled on average 57% of their buying journey.[51] The buyer group shares a brief with all the potential solution providers that includes detailed technical requirements and a request for a price. With this type of opportunity, suppliers are asked to fulfil an existing and defined need.

An invitation to participate in an RFP process should prompt sales and technical experts in the supplier organisation to conduct a go/no-go discussion, especially if this is the first time your organisation has heard of this customer opportunity. Choosing to participate, or not, is not an easy decision. On the surface, it seems like a business opportunity just waiting to be seized: a prospective client calls you and is ready to spend money on a clearly defined problem they want to solve. This type of incoming business opportunity could be seen as **low-hanging fruit**.

There are, however, several challenges to be aware of when you choose to participate in this process. The solution requirements could have been shaped by a different supplier, which places them in a better position to win the deal; the requested solution and features may not be what you would have recommended in the same context; even worse, what has been asked for will not help the customer improve business outcomes. In addition, a thorough and professional answer tailored to the customer context requires a lot of time and effort and is unlikely to have a good pay-off. This type of buying method pushes a supplier into a reactive product-selling approach, which leads to a price and features comparison – possibly leaving only a low margin and commoditised deal on the table. Technical experts who have to support the commercial teams in the context of fulfilling a need are also often cornered into a reactive role in which they have to service every request in the pursuit of winning the deal.

There are two questions which can help to review priorities and check whether the requested services and activities will increase the likelihood of reaching commercial outcomes:

1. **Does the requested solution lead to improved customer outcomes?**

2. **Is there a change agent within the buying stakeholder group?**

Let's address these two questions in turn.

If you believe the requested solution and features are potentially addressing only a symptom of the customer's business problem rather than a root cause, then the first thing to check is whether the customer is open to reviewing their buying criteria. This can lead to two options (irrespective of whether the customer likes the fact that your organisation is looking after their longer-term client interests and outcomes): they either agree to reset the buying criteria or there is no appetite to change the direction because, after all, it was already hard to get to this point.

If the latter happens, as a supplier you can respectfully decline to put your offer forward and share a clear reason as to why you are doing so, especially if there are limited resources for several opportunities. You will be remembered as a supplier who is looking after the interests of the customer and not only in it for the money. It is not uncommon that your organisation will be contacted again, especially if the problem continues to exist after the customer has tried the wrong solution from a different supplier.

Of course, it is not necessarily black and white; sometimes there can be additional compelling arguments to participate in an RFP. A foot in the door can help you create additional opportunities, winning revenue means you can invest more in your business, and/or a requested solution may be better than doing nothing at all.

To answer the second question, you need to check whether you have access to a change agent in the customer organisation to drive change in your desired direction. You need one or more change agents to help refocus the problem or review the solution and take the initiative to help create buyer consensus around a new approach.

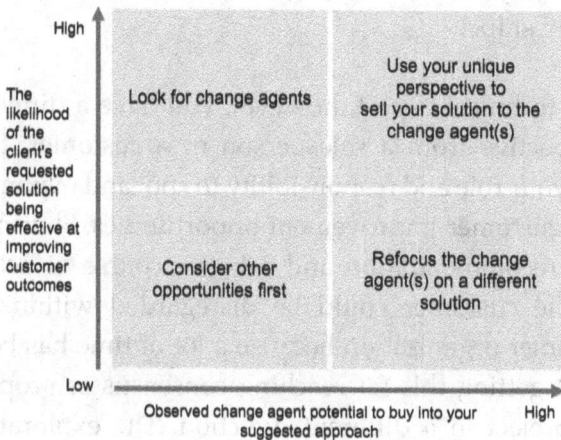

The customer opportunity evaluation matrix

As a technical expert, you may be involved in supporting the delivery of a client project that has already been scoped or launched. In many ways, this can be compared to the context of fulfilling a need: there is an agreed-upon commercial and delivery framework that you are asked to operate in. From your technical perspective, maybe there could be a better way forward to achieve longer-term customer improvement. Is the timing right and will the type of customer improvement opportunity warrant the additional change effort? You do not want to unnecessarily derail the project, as this could go against the buyer expectation of you being easy to work with.

It is tempting to take the easy road and entirely comply with all the requirements and parameters defined by the customer and/or your colleagues. Especially if the buying or implementation journey is well underway, it takes courage and resilience to turn a sailing ship.

As a technical expert, however, you have a different perspective from a salesperson or a customer. It is also your role and responsibility to spot and maximise new customer improvement opportunities. Sharing a new recommendation and a better course of action for the customer could be disregarded within the customer organisation because a lot of time has been spent getting this far-reaching consensus or scoping the project in a different direction. The exploration and discussion of pros and cons of pursuing a new

This is not a sequential process. If the buying process were linear, sequential and structured, then it would be clear where and when technical experts could work together with salespeople to help add commercial value and win new business or grow existing accounts. In a predictable process, it would also suffice to detail clear roles and responsibilities and define the potential hand-off points between different internal stakeholders so that everyone knew when to play their part. Every resource would be optimally used without duplication or overlap.

None of this is possible, however, because 'linear', 'structured' and 'predictable' are not characteristics of a typical buying process. Buying a new service or product from a supplier can also be happening in parallel in an existing partnership or in the execution of a client project for a different department. Because buying is not a linear nor a predictable process, the key for technical experts is to understand what questions need to be answered and where there are opportunities to fulfil buyer expectations that drive loyalty and growth.

As explained, in the context of fulfilling a need, you have less control and impact on the direction and outcomes. A new customer improvement opportunity on how to run a better business should, ideally, be shared before the (prospective) customer reaches out to you as a supplier. By creating both a new customer improvement opportunity and authentic customer improvement opportunity will, however, be valuable in itself. Even if the project does not progress any further afterwards, it serves as learning for future implementations.

Creating a need

Customers are more likely to reset their buying criteria when they are confronted with surprising information about their business. Suppliers who bring a new perspective on solving an (unknown) business problem are in a much better position to control the direction and the outcome when they create a client need.

The art of creating a need is to expose a new perspective on a business issue and to make a case for change with rational and emotional arguments to compel the customer to act. When you prepare a strong, unique and valuable customer improvement message, it will create authentic urgency within the customer organisation. Instead of picking the low-hanging fruit, you **plant your own fruit tree**, which is a more impactful and sustainable growth opportunity.

Armed with a greater understanding of what increases the chances of driving change and winning new commercial opportunities, as a technical expert you should be in a position to constructively challenge and / or shape priorities which are worth pursuing. When a project or implementation comes to an end, it creates a window of opportunity to suggest the next steps on the journey. At that moment, a technical expert has a lot of influence on the direction that is taken afterwards. Even without any new project or upsell opportunity, this will be perceived as customer improvement. Technical experts who contribute beyond the standard implementation brief in that moment seize the greatest opportunity to impact commercial outcomes.

Process: Reaching new commercial outcomes

Choosing which customer improvement opportunities to engage in and setting the right priorities are key to optimising resources such as people and time. The second important consideration when reviewing your strategy is to understand how you can play a role in the process to drive impact. It is important to note that there are two elements to consider: the sales and delivery process, which is typically happening in your own supplier organisation, and the buying process, which is happening in the customer organisation.

The sales and delivery process

Technical experts may be brought in as presales advisors to help win a deal or deliver their technical urgency to solve the problem, you can take control over the buying agenda. The tasks of a buyer group are likely to change focus to something resembling the examples below:

- **Business challenge validation**: 'I didn't know I had this problem! We need to explore its importance in the broader context of our business priorities.'

- **Stakeholder identification**: 'I need to get people involved who will be impacted by a solution which solves this newly identified problem.'

- **Buying criteria (re)setting**: 'We like the sound of this, but we may need to agree/review our buying criteria first.'

- **Review of ROI on (new) commercial relationship**: 'Are there other good-value-for-money comparable solutions out there in the market?'

- **Mobilising towards consensus and change**: 'Let's agree on the resources needed to solve this problem; every day we wait is a wasted opportunity.'

A strong customer improvement message created by salespeople and/or technical experts can speed up the change process because the urgency is felt by the customer. The question you need to ask yourself is: 'How can I equip the customer with the information they need to anticipate questions, objections and next steps to proceed with this opportunity?' Where are the areas of risk in the change? What will making a change impact or disrupt (eg people, processes, activities, systems)? Are there ways to manage and minimise those anticipated disruptions? If so, how?

Finally, is there a way to enable the buyer group with a clear plan and timelines to stay on track? Customers want suppliers to make the buying process easier not harder. Technical experts can formulate these questions and offer valuable insight into the change process within the buyer group.

Plan: Formulating clear steps and activities

Before you move into clear actions and steps to drive a new customer opportunity forward, it is important to review your COSMOS preparation in a more holistic way. You could first score the effectiveness of your preparation using a diagram (see figure below) and then decide where to focus and which actions to take to improve your chances to make a commercial impact, thinking about what you can do yourself versus where you need help from other teams and departments. This will also help to share goals with other team members because it highlights areas that need more focus or where you feel you have a possible strength.

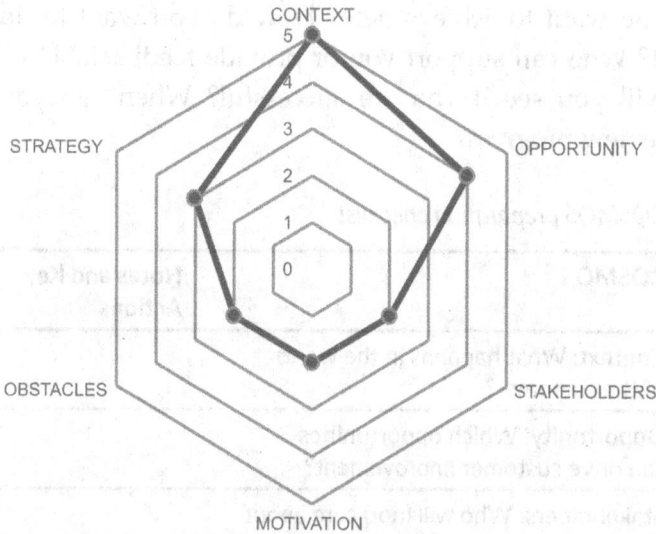

COSMOS preparation hexagon

The figure illustrates that there may be solid knowledge about the context and potential customer improvement opportunities, but we don't yet have visibility of who we need to engage with, what their motivators are to embark on the change or which objections we may encounter. The strategy will focus on looking for the key priorities and seeking information on stakeholders and their motivation to buy in to the potential customer improvement.

The below table can be used to capture your notes and key actions to increase understanding of each section of COSMOS. Keep the following questions in mind when you're completing each section: What do you want to achieve here? How do you want to do it? Who can support you or provide feedback? How will you see if you are successful? When can you review progress?

COSMOS preparation checklist

COSMOS	Notes and Key Actions
Context: What happens in the world of the customer?	
Opportunity: Which opportunities can drive customer improvement?	
Stakeholders: Who will (not) care about the≈customer improvement opportunity?	
Motivation: What motivates change or no change?	
Obstacles: Which obstacles/objections hinder the journey towards change?	
Strategy: Where to focus to realise commercial outcomes?	

PART THREE
PUTTING IT INTO ACTION

Part Three focuses on *how* you can aspire to customer improvement. I will explain in more detail three behavioural AIMs (Anticipate needs, Inspire with insight and Mobilise change) which, if combined and put into action, will support this process. These outcomes build on what I have learned from the application and research outlined in *The Challenger Sale, The Challenger Customer* and *The Jolt Effect.*[53,54,55]

Although I have chosen to explain 'anticipate needs' first, there is no chronological order to these three behavioural outcomes. Any could come first, depending on what you are trying to achieve in a given part of a process and what type of stakeholder you are interacting with. They are all connected and equally important to drive commercial impact and take control of your ongoing commercial development.

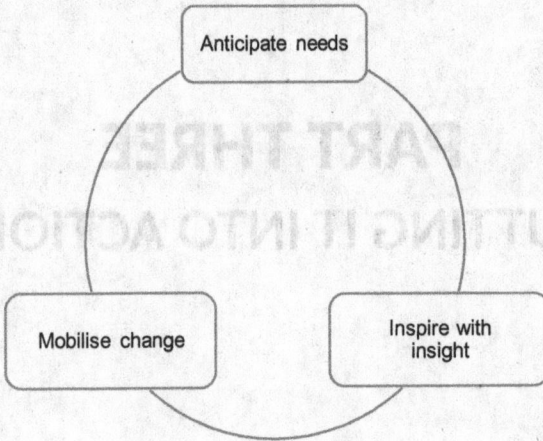

*Connecting **AIM** outcomes*

Developing commercial capability is unlikely to happen through a 'do it once and it is completed' approach without focusing on a broader work context and personal aspirations. In this part I will suggest some activities to help make customer improvement an integral part of the personal development of technical experts. I will also offer concrete tips to help realise your customer improvement goals.

I will go into more detail about the role leaders can play to help technical experts improve their commercial capabilities and look at some concrete ways to get started as soon as possible. Implementing AIM and COSMOS does not have to be a long-term goal: with the right mindset and the right people, companies can get started today. I will also share some of the findings from my international research to help understand which values and personality traits seem to correlate highly with the expected AIM behaviours and support businesses in preparing for the most relevant aspects of COSMOS.

Finally, I will touch on the concept of employee experience and how understanding this as well as using new technology and AI can help improve the chances of unlocking commercial potential and capability development.

10
Anticipate Needs

I t is important to remember that commercial stars are not born. Anyone with a minimum of commercial potential aligned to B2B sales and buyer context requirements can apply and develop commercial or customer improvement behaviours. It is a matter of learning to anticipate what is needed to drive towards customer improvement, then setting the right priorities and goals, committing to these goals and reflecting on what has been learned to improve your approach. As is the case with every new skill: practice makes perfect.

'Anticipating' implies that you are preparing your reaction to something before it happens. In this chapter I will share how technical experts can develop their commercial development capabilities in such a way that they will become better at helping the customer. Technical experts need to take a broader perspective than they are used to, to see customer improvement across silos. Along with anticipating the **needs of the customers**, it is important to anticipate your own **personal development needs**.

Your personal development needs

The previous chapters covered several opportunities for technical experts to drive commercial impact (directly or indirectly) and impact the buyer experience. Learning on the job has more impact on your performance than learning from formal training. Starting to look for new experiences is the right way to help you develop your commercial capability, but it will not be enough. It is even more important to extract useful insights from your chosen on-the-job learning activities. People often find this difficult. There are seven key questions you can use before, during and after your customer improvement activities to help you develop your commercial capability.

1. Why am I doing this?

What compels you to increase your commercial capability level and maximise your commercial potential? What is your purpose? Do you want to become more commercially focused because you would like increased commercial responsibilities, or are you convinced that you will become more employable if you have a more commercially rounded approach and a greater understanding of how you can impact organisational outcomes? Whatever the answer is, understanding what's in it for you is a key starting point to giving yourself a clear purpose, target and/or desired outcome.

2. What type of commercial improvement activity should I look for?

It is worth taking a shot at describing your chosen customer improvement in a succinct way. It helps you test how the technical expertise or solution (services and/or products) links to specific customer objectives you want to focus on. In addition to formulating your customer improvement opportunity, as described in Part Two, you should reflect on the following questions:

- Will you choose to do something entirely new, and will it help you develop a new experience, or are you building on something you have done in the past?

- Do you want the customer improvement activity to be visible, or would you rather continue to work behind the scenes?

- Are there any potential sources of conflict (eg competing priorities)? If so, what do you need to do to reduce them, along with stress or negative impact?

These questions will help you make the most out of this activity and prevent you from just throwing yourself in at the deep end.

3. Where am I now and where do I want to be?

It is important to think about the gap between where you are now and where you want to be. How can you make your success visible, gradual and realistic? Where are you today in terms of commercial capability and contributions? You should choose activities which stretch you but not so much that it becomes too uncomfortable and/or hinders you from navigating them successfully.

There will be areas that will be more natural for technical experts to work on based on a preferred working style, and other areas can be successfully tackled with help from people with complementing profiles and strengths. Communication around the COSMOS preparation checklist and identifying strengths and development areas in the light of your commercial AIM will be helpful tools to use as a source of inspiration to answer this question.

4. How will I get to my outcome?

Coming up with an answer to this question requires you to understand your role and responsibilities in both the supplier and customer buyer process. What challenges do you think you will encounter? What resources are available now, during and after the activity? What is your approach to the learning experience and what do you need to get out of this task or activity?

5. Who can help me?

Even if you are not new to commercial activities and/or coming up with new customer improvement opportunities, it is likely you will need some support from others to help drive your ideas to a successful conclusion. Who could support you? Are there technical experts who could be commercial role models as you work out how to develop your activities? Can certain people share their approach and feedback with you? Looking for feedback from people with different roles and experiences can help enrich your learning experience and offer you valuable perspective to develop your commercial capability. You can share where you have progressed or where you are stuck in your COSMOS preparation or where you could use the skills of people who can complement your views and/or natural preferences. The process of creating and driving new customer improvement activities will likely be more effective if worked on and reviewed by people who add different perspectives and additional support.

6. Is now the time to reflect and ask for feedback?

Being exposed to the right kind of development activities is important and valuable; however, just going through an experience is not enough. What matters is whether you are extracting the right learnings from the activities. This will make you perform even better in the future. What surprised you about the learning experience? What did (not) meet your expectations? Which skills and behaviours did you display most effectively during the experience? If you were to repeat the experience, what would you do differently?

A learning opportunity seen through your own lens is important, and being open to seeking feedback from other people will account for an even bigger part of your capability development. You could ask a simple question: 'What should I start to do, keep doing, do more of or stop doing in the future to increase my commercial capability and impact?'

7. Who can benefit from my learning?

As a technical expert in one area, there are probably opportunities for you to teach others about your learning experience, especially if you work across different silos. Is there anyone you can share your learnings with? This last question is often overlooked. It makes you a part of other people's learning, just as you made other people part of your learning.

Once you have answered these seven key questions and you have one or more specific customer improvement opportunities in mind, you can create your own personal goal to help track progress. The example below can help you capture your customer improvement objective as part of your development plan in an effective way and anticipate what is required to stay relevant and adapt to changing (personal/customer) needs or context requirements. It is important to describe specific and realistic action steps and where possible include realistic developments between where you are now and where you want to be.

Personal goal planner

	Notes and actions
Personal goal: What do I want to achieve?	
Action steps: How do I want to do it?	
Support: Who can help and provide feedback?	
Success measures: How will I see if I have been successful?	
Review: When is my next checkpoint?	
Upskilling others: Who can benefit from my learning?	

The need of the customer

Employees who communicate and collaborate across silos to provide integrated solutions for customers create value for their organisations. This finding comes from research conducted with hundreds of executives across many organisations. The authors, Edmondson, Jang and Casciaro, present a set of practices that facilitates cross-silo leadership, which can be learned and developed.[56]

Following this research, ideas were developed on how people can work across silos. In this section I will look at the most relevant ideas that technical experts can apply to anticipate customer improvement needs, which in many ways will imply both operating in and looking beyond their own silo.

Ask questions that facilitate a broader perspective

Most companies still focus on creating well-oiled functional processes and tools to execute on functional priorities. Many leaders and teams continue to focus on solutions from within one silo and perfecting these without looking at the overall picture of what needs to happen to improve customer outcomes in a more holistic way. Aspiring to customer improvement which can make buying easier and identify risks and alternatives to increase longer-term business impact means we need to look beyond our typical sales and marketing approaches and review broader end-to-end processes. These opportunities can reside in project or product implementation, or in the legal, accounting or aftercare elements of the process.

The first skill technical experts can apply to understand the broader perspective is to ask good open questions to discover where there may be opportunities for customer improvement. As Kevin Kelly states in his book *The Inevitable*:

> 'A good question is the seed of innovation—
> in science, technology, art, politics, and
> business... A good question is a probe, a
> "what if" scenario. A good question cannot
> be predicted. Asking good questions may be
> the last job machines will learn to do. A good
> question is what humans are for.'[57]

Asking good open questions to understand someone else's perspective is something people can choose to learn and practise. It means empathising with someone else's needs and actively demonstrating curiosity beyond your technical domain. Curious employees who ask the right types of questions build broad networks that **span boundaries** across disparate parts of the company.[58] This helps organisations to gain a competitive advantage.

Often, new joiners in a company get introduced to people in different departments but those meetings don't necessarily drive better cross-department collaborations that lead to customer improvement opportunities. Examples of questions you could ask to explore broader connections and perspectives across the organisation include:

- 'From your perspective, how can my technical contribution impact the broader customer journey in a positive way?'

- 'In what way could my contribution help to achieve a higher return or customer impact?'

- 'From where you sit, how can you see my technical contribution potentially derailing or losing traction in driving change towards improved customer outcomes?'

Act as a cultural broker

As a technical expert, can you think of opportunities that you can personally act on to connect people and solutions across typical company divides? How can your unique perspective help you come up with a view or solution that nobody else has thought of?

REFLECTION: CULTURAL DIFFERENCES

In many global companies with headquarters in the US or UK, the most senior leadership positions get occupied by US or UK leaders from a homogenous group. Important business decisions about product design, sales and marketing do not always align to the expectations of international and multicultural employees and/or customers. 'It works for us so it will work for them' is the underlying assumption.

I come from a mixed family (my mother's side is Portuguese and my father's side is Belgian) and have witnessed the misunderstandings that can arise from a relatively small cultural difference. This has led me to generally try to represent the non-typical central voice: multicultural stakeholders and customers in different markets. I often acted as a culture broker in meetings and projects. What was potentially overlooked? How would different international stakeholders react to the suggested timing, solution or approach?

Try to think what type of diversity you bring to the perspectives of people you work with and don't be afraid to ask the non-obvious or different questions from your (different) perspective.

Being a cultural broker means you facilitate interactions between people and teams who have different sets of assumptions, values and norms. The original cultural broker research from Sujin Jang was applied to multinationals, but the author posited that it could also apply to different functional or organisational cultures.[59]

The author identified two distinct roles of cultural brokerage: those who help colleagues work around cultural differences ('bridges') and those who connect colleagues with one another to build lasting relationships ('adhesives').

- A *bridge* allows others to collaborate across silos with little disruption to their daily routine. They do this by taking care of the cross-silo work on behalf of others in such a way that employees can continue working as they would within their own silo. This kind of cultural brokerage is efficient because it lets disparate parties work around differences without investing in learning the other side's perspective or changing how they work. It is especially valuable for one-off collaborations or when the company is under intense time pressure to deliver results.

- An *adhesive* connects colleagues and helps them work directly with one another, rather than acting as a bridge between them. They sow the seed for further productive relationships to flourish, independent of the cultural broker.

Offering your help in cross-functional working groups that look at capturing perspectives for new products, solutions or customer processes will be one way to achieve this.

11
Inspire With Insight

The second important behavioural outcome for technical experts is to inspire with insight. Technical experts can often be enthusiastic about the technical expertise and jargon but have less focus on how to influence and sell new ideas and approaches.

Selling customer improvement

Selling an idea for customer improvement is more likely to appeal to technical experts than selling to win a deal or obtain more money. Many people have a negative view of the sales profession. The typical stereotypes are that salespeople are pushy, think only about their bonus and/or want to sell things customers don't really need. By having salespeople and technical experts focus on gaining competitive advantage through customer improvement, the sales process can provide them with personal satisfaction because most people think positively of helping others to solve their problems. Of course, this approach will also directly and indirectly impact retention and growth: a win-win situation.

Customers can learn about customer improvement opportunities from suppliers, from colleagues and from third-party consultants or experts. Learning about potential business improvements and taking control over consensus creation within a buyer group are two key goals that technical experts need to focus on because they will be of special interest to Mobilizers. We have seen that Mobilizers (as defined in *The Challenger Customer* research) are people who care deeply about change to improve the organisation and about ways to create consensus around key business improvement objectives.[60] Anyone within the sales organisation should consider ways to help Mobilizers successfully fulfil these two critical goals.

The Mobilizer within a customer organisation needs to be equipped with the content and tools to create a shared objective in the buyer group and be able to answer challenging questions when the supplier is not present. The buyer group needs to learn about new possibilities to drive better outcomes. Less is more when it comes to deciding what you share, and how you share it, with the Mobilizer.

Too often, suppliers make the mistake of creating a lot of strong content which informs customers about an issue but does not drive urgency. Sometimes, when sharing a problem, the supplier is not able to help with it, resulting in frustration or other competitors benefiting from a commercial opportunity. Even if the content is relevant, it can easily disappear out of sight between all the other available content and information in the marketplace. How can a supplier inspire potential customers on new customer improvement ideas? In the following paragraphs we will cover different techniques to sell change or customer improvement.

The persuasive power of a reframe

Reframing is one of the most effective persuasive techniques and a powerful communication tool that can also be used outside the sales context.[61] When speaking to a customer within any commercial context, it may become clear that they have a limited understanding of a problem that is being discussed. This means that you, as the professional brought in to help find a solution, may need to first enhance the customer's understanding of the problem. Presenting a solution without reaching a workable level of understanding of the scope of the problem may result in the solution being declined or misunderstood or in setting an unrealistic level of expectation, which will eventually lead to a dissatisfied customer.

An example may make this easier to understand. A senior manager in a customer organisation attends a meeting with a salesperson and a technical expert and comes with a clear and precise ask. It is tempting for each salesperson to present a solution to the client problem – people want to help solve problems – but if the technical expert realises that the ask does not match the customer need, a reframing approach will lead to better outcomes. Although there is a problem to be solved, the customer has not yet identified the root cause of this problem but rather one of the symptoms that result from this underlying root cause.

At this point the commercial team (salesperson and technical expert) must choose between being compliant with what the customer is asking for or trying to shift the customer's understanding of the situation so that they see the underlying root problem. The first approach may lead to a quicker business deal, but the results will probably disappoint. As a result, follow-up work may be required to come up with better results, but this may still not solve the problem and the relationship with the customer will become strained.

The second approach – of shifting or reframing the customer's understanding of the situation or problem – will, if properly applied, lead to better results and a higher chance of a long-term relationship with a satisfied customer, but the technical expert will have to move carefully to avoid being perceived as aggressive or defiant, which will also hurt the relationship with the customer. A great way to start such a reorientation discussion is by asking probing questions. These will enable the technical expert to double-check that they have fully understood the client's needs (rather than their asks).

Good probing questions will slowly lead the customer away from their own conclusions and carefully guide them towards understanding the problem, as seen through the eyes of the technical expert. Once the customer is willing to consider that they may have overlooked facts and, in so doing, have reached an incomplete conclusion (the wrong ask), it is time to reframe their ask.

At this point the technical expert will have to refer to a technical framework: a commonly accepted and scientifically valid way of looking at a problem. These frameworks can vary enormously, depending on the nature of the customer's business, and may come from fields as diverse as HR, IT, Finance, R&D, Engineering or Technology.

The technical expert can use their knowledge of the framework to formulate probing questions that will slowly draw the customer in, which 'anchors' the customer around a new way of looking at the problem.

The customer will then have stepped away from their initial ask and will be in a position where they can be made to see a new ask that matches their need. This process of reframing customer expectations takes some skill. Moving the customer away from their initial ask too slowly and carefully may result in a customer unwilling to adopt a new perspective; moving a customer too quickly and abruptly may result in a customer feeling threatened and digging in their heels.

When the reframe is brought about successfully, the customer will have gained a new and better understanding of their needs, while the teaching role of the technical expert will have increased the trust in the relationship between the customer and the commercial team. It is interesting to see the technical expert as a teacher, because in some ways the reframing technique bears a striking resemblance to the Socratic method. The Greek philosopher Socrates was known for using questions to show people a contradiction in their reasoning and then asking additional questions to help them to develop a new position in which the contradiction no longer existed. Two and a half thousand years on, this technique is still successfully used to teach customers to see new insights and close better business deals.

Building reframes

The reframe is built from combining the anchor and ask, as illustrated in the figure below.

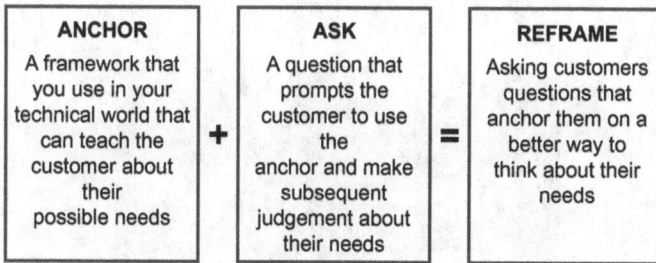

ANCHOR		ASK		REFRAME
A framework that you use in your technical world that can teach the customer about their possible needs	**+**	A question that prompts the customer to use the anchor and make subsequent judgement about their needs	**=**	Asking customers questions that anchor them on a better way to think about their needs

Building reframes

Anchors come in different forms and can be explored on a **root cause tree**, which breaks the client's specific problem (at the top of the diagram on the figure below) into different causes.

The tree can help to see the bigger picture when the client is too detail-focused or deepen their understanding when the client sees only the bigger picture. It can help to see what can be looked at to obtain a more complete perspective of potential root causes of a given observation.

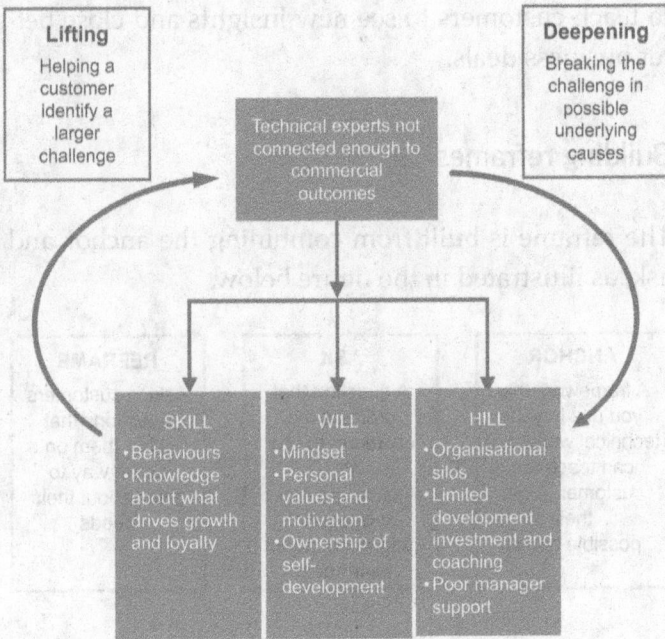

Lifting	Technical experts not connected enough to commercial outcomes	Deepening
Helping a customer identify a larger challenge		Breaking the challenge in possible underlying causes

SKILL	WILL	HILL
• Behaviours • Knowledge about what drives growth and loyalty	• Mindset • Personal values and motivation • Ownership of self-development	• Organisational silos • Limited development investment and coaching • Poor manager support

Root cause tree: Why technical experts don't connect enough to commercial outcomes

Different types of anchors can be used, such as sharing extremes on a spectrum, sharing trade-offs or giving options. Examples of each can be seen in the list below:

1. **Trade-off**

   Anchor: 'When customising solutions to specific customer needs, we need to look at trade-offs, such as proven business outcomes and ease of implementation (cost, time, quality).'

Ask: 'Which criteria should get most of your focus now?'

2. Extremes/Spectrum

Anchor: 'Many organisations choose to hire technical experts purely on past experience and proven technical skills. On the other hand, we can see more forward-looking hiring that considers learning mindset, commercial potential and ownership of development to stay aligned to future business needs.'

Ask: 'Where do you see yourself on this spectrum?'

3. Options/Scenarios

Anchor: 'We can choose self-paced e-learning which helps people learn at their own pace and save time, or we can choose to run virtual workshops which allow people to learn from colleagues and interaction, or a combination of both.'

Ask: 'Which of these options would work best for the technical experts in your organisation?'

Selling change and overcoming customer indecision

Successful salespeople need to know when and how to sell change and overcome customer indecision in any given sales process.[62] The below visual represents a simplified sales process of three key phases: a customer needs to be sold to the idea of changing what they are doing (or not doing) now in other words 'their status quo'. Secondly there needs to be a shared vision between the salesperson and the customer on how to achieve better outcomes using a new product, solution or service. Finally, the customer needs to agree to purchase the new solution or product. Depending on the industry, the organisation, the complexity of the buying process and the type of products and services sold, this process could take from a couple of days up to several years.

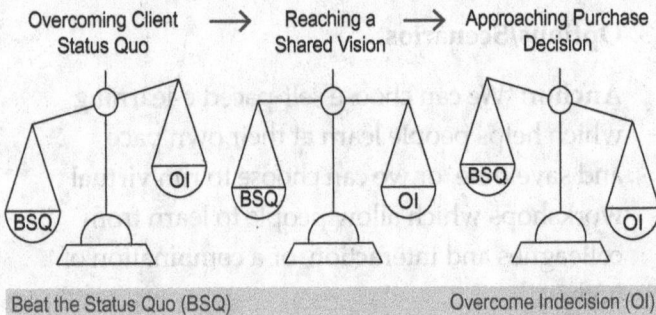

| Overcoming Client Status Quo | → | Reaching a Shared Vision | → | Approaching Purchase Decision |

Beat the Status Quo (BSQ)   Overcome Indecision (OI)

Overcoming the status quo of the client on its own isn't sufficient, because indecision can surface at different levels of intensity throughout the entire sales process.[63]

To sell change towards customer improvement (or beating the status quo of the customer) and to overcome customer indecision you need to gain trust by showing your understanding of the customer's context. You cannot just walk up to someone and say,

'Hey, I think there is a better way of doing what you are doing now.' They will think you are arrogant. Customers take advice from salespeople or technical experts they trust and deem to be credible. As a technical expert, you first need to think about how you can earn the right to share a different view on their world and way of approaching things.

My COSMOS preparation framework will help you to dive into the world of the customer, understand the results that different stakeholders need to achieve and see how key trends and issues may be impacting them in the pursuit of better business outcomes. You can demonstrate credibility by showing you have an interest in their world and that you care about their success. The purpose is to establish trust and credibility through a collaborative conversation. A potential pitfall here is sharing everything you know about the world of the customer, which may come across as a laundry list of technical issues that you may not be able to solve.

To successfully beat the status quo of the customer, we need to try to identify an incorrect belief or assumption about the way a customer sees (or does not see) a problem that is impacting their business. When you sell change you should ideally expose the flaws in the way they look at their problem. The aim is to identify a customer improvement opportunity or underappreciated business challenge based on your experience, technical knowledge or external research. Avoid sharing too many irrelevant facts which dilute the key message and do not create urgency to act.

If a stakeholder within the customer organisation just thinks, 'this is interesting' after hearing about your new customer improvement insight, it is unlikely they will act on anything. Is there anything intriguing or does this new insight have magnitude, a business case and an impact on the organisation? When trying to beat the status quo of the customer and sell change towards customer improvement, you should also appeal to how the left brain captures information, analyses concepts and processes logical thoughts. Change does not happen if there is no impact, so it is key for you to demonstrate how big the impact can be on the organisation or on the stakeholder(s). A potential pitfall is that you focus too much on the benefits of a new approach or a rosy future. No facts, too many facts or no logical structure to your facts are all ways to confuse your audience and reduce the impact.

To effectively sell change you also need to appeal to the right side of the brain, which looks at how things work or why they exist. It can see the bigger picture and is forward-thinking. It has the capacity to actively imagine. Is there a relevant story that your audience can relate to? Are there anecdotes or examples which people can relate to emotionally? There is probably an abundance of stories of moments in the end-to-end sales and delivery process which need to be reviewed. People connect to change when they understand there is a human impact. How can you demonstrate this and what is the pain caused by not changing? In any case, it should be bigger than the pain of changing. What you need to be mindful of when creating emotional impact is that it cannot be unrealistic or over the top because this may then trigger customer indecision or inaction

---

REFLECTION: THREE KEY ISSUES WITH SELLING CHANGE

Respectfully telling a (prospective) customer that they may have an incorrect approach to dealing with a business issue is not easy. I have helped many people understand the key ingredients of a story that can help sell change. Three issues frequently surfaced during these trainings:

1. The focus of the story often quickly shifted to the supplier's products or services. As the world of the customer was overlooked, the result was a traditional product-selling approach and the belief that, 'This problem is costing you money and our solution will fix this.'

2. Traditional relationship builders as defined in the original Challenger research felt uncomfortable with the tension this approach could potentially create.[64] In their eyes, telling the client that they are wrong is a way of damaging the client relationship. If done in a respectful way, based on trust and credibility, however, the client will most likely value this different perspective on their business. According to Gartner research in 2019, offering a unique, critical

perspective on improving the client's business is a key driver of account growth.

3. Those who incorporated all the ingredients of a good story forgot basic conversation and diagnostic skills. Instead of a two-way dialogue with natural pauses and an opportunity for questions from both parties, the story became too mechanical and scripted – or even annoying.

Creating a powerful story flow to sell customer improvement is not easy and can be time-consuming. The preparation should happen before the interaction with the (potential) customer. If it is done well, the person you speak to will feel an urgency to act and be prompted to move things along in the buying organisation. A good story, focused on selling change towards customer improvement with relevant anecdotes, can be formed by bringing together different technical experts who can anticipate different needs and questions from a diverse buying stakeholder group. When possible, commercial messages should be created centrally with different experts and outside help (organisations such as Challenger Performance Optimization Inc provide messaging support aligned to a proven Challenger sale choreography)[65] to support technical experts and sales teams. Although achieving customer improvement will appeal to a large group of technical experts, most people feel uncomfortable with change and the tensions this may bring. Every person will react differently to a new customer improvement idea and the change it implies.

It is quite common that salespeople receive sales enablement tools to help them be successful in the sales process; for example, objection handling, ROI stories, implementation examples, anecdotes and use cases. These types of content need to also be provided to help a change agent in a customer organisation create agreement on a new vision in their organisation. The supporting tools should focus on making change agents self-sufficient at dealing with different topics and questions in the buyer group. For these to be relevant and usable by a change agent, however, they need to be repurposed to become customer-facing, supplier-neutral and have a focus on the nature of the business problem and a potential new way forward. We also know from the JOLT research that high-performing salespeople control the flow of information shared with prospective customers and offer relevant recommendations to move the customer away from indecision or the fear of messing up when embarking on a new approach.[66] From this Jolt research, which analysed several million sales conversations against win rates of deals, it became clear that successfully adding JOLT skills in sales conversations (Judging customer Indecision, Offering your recommendations, Limiting the customer exploration and Taking risk of the table aligned to change and purchase) can significantly increase high performance. Techniques to overcome indecision currently don't get much focus in sales training programmes. The authors of the Jolt research support organisations on how to effectively apply these skills, based on their latest research.[67]

Technical experts can actively support the creation of content and the structure and ingredients of a great story towards customer improvement. By understanding the purpose of these tools and the pitfalls that can happen along the way from creation to message delivery, technical experts can offer feedback or help increase the impact.

What is certain is that emotions drive most decision-making processes and an audience retains information longer and more efficiently when they are spoken to in story form. If you want your presentation, pitch or recommendation to be remembered and your audience to take the desired action, you will be more successful when you use storytelling.

A lot has been written about storytelling. There are many research-based recipes for successful storytelling and effectively changing people's ideas and behaviours, but asking every technical expert to figure this out by themself may be risky. Good storytelling that leads to change is hard and will remain a uniquely human skill. Storytellers can never forget the role they play in their own stories and need to be very aware of customer's signals linked to them preferring their status quo or indecision. I have seen many people struggle with this and it is one of the areas where a greater focus on time and development could lead to immediate customer and business improvement.

Adapting to different communication styles

When you need to prepare for a message to land effectively, you need to understand how to balance facts and stories, details and the bigger picture. Although all of these can be ingredients in a compelling story that can help you sell change, how you balance them depends on who you are communicating to.

In your eyes, your story may be perfect and compelling, but it still may not land as you expected. This is probably because you did not think through how to deliver the message in a way that was aligned to the communication style of your audience. Everyone has a preferred way of absorbing information. The social styles model created by Robert and Dorothy Bolton is a simple typology framework that can be used to help people understand the different preferences of communication in a professional context. The four types of styles are explained in the table below.[68]

If you are preparing to communicate with a key stakeholder and share a robust detailed and factual story, this may perfectly resonate with the communication style of an 'analytic', but a 'driver' may completely zone out because they prefer a message delivered at pace with a focus on outcomes.

People do not necessarily have only one approach – they can have a primary and secondary communication

	Expressives 'Let me tell you my ideas about this.'	Drivers 'Let's take action on this.'	Analytics 'Let me think about this.'	Amiables 'Let's meet to discuss this.'
Their characteristics	Enthusiastic	Candid	Accurate	Cooperative
	Persuasive	Results-oriented	Organised	Diplomatic
	Spontaneous	Strong-willed	Thorough	Loyal
	Outgoing	Decisive	Logical	Dependable
	Ambitious	Independent	Systematic	Supportive
Their interests	Ideas and possibilities	Outcomes	Facts	Relationships and communication
What they have questions about	Why	What	How	Who
Their pace	Fast	Fast	Slower	Slower
	Spontaneous	Decisive	Systematic	Relaxed
What they want you to support	Their dream	Their conclusions	Their process	Their feelings

Social Styles at work model by Robert Bolton and Dorothy Grover Bolton style or preference. As with many other personality theories that use categories based on researched personality types, there are limitations because people do not exist in just four flavours or styles. If you have limited information about the stakeholders you will encounter, it is important to review the checklist and see whether your message can be tailored to appeal to more than just one communication style.

12
Mobilise Change Towards Customer Improvement

C hange can be painful and even the best customer improvement opportunity could stall in your supplier organisation before it gets presented to a customer. In this section, I will cover the third key behavioural outcome: to mobilise change more quickly and more effectively. Technical experts have several opportunities to mobilise resources and people for change. They can do so at different moments of the end-to-end sales and delivery process, as described in the strategy section of the COSMOS framework.

Enabling change within your organisation, or in a (prospective) customer, is not an individual sport. It will not work without a plan to deal with specific stakeholders who need to be brought along on the journey. To make things happen, you need to start looking for internal colleagues who can team up with you to help drive change. You do this by scanning for people who can help drive impact or broker customer improvement across different parts of the organisation. Externally, you need to look at ways to enable the Mobilizers and find tactics to reduce the negative impact of blockers. You also need to resist shying away from providing clear recommendations and an answer to the 'Now what?' question, because it anticipates next steps and, as a result, drives change more quickly and effectively. We will cover this in more detail at the end of this chapter.

Expand your impact through network scanning

One of the challenges of working across divides in organisations has to do with the perception of who is connected to whom beyond the formal organisation chart. As a technical expert without direct impact on clients or sales outcomes, you need to find the right connections to drive change internally before you can impact customer outcomes.

This ability to perceive the web of connections in an organisation is important because the more technical experts can broaden their vision of where the interesting opportunities are or where the important intersections might be, the easier it is to work across silos. Tiziana Casciaro and colleagues found that people do not understand exactly who is connected to whom in a network, a concept they call 'elemental' perception.[69] For example, if I know two individuals in the organisation, I tend to assume they know each other, even if this is not the case. Elemental perception can block our progress. A 'holistic' perception of a network involves determining who is central. This makes it easier to see which colleagues are well connected and which work on the periphery. Luckily, most people have relatively little trouble identifying this.

With this holistic perception, we understand who our go-to person for information is. Technical experts can develop their network perception by asking questions and working out who is central in an organisation and who makes decisions. This can help progress customer improvement opportunities across silos to benefit the end customer.

Unite internal stakeholders around customer improvement

Selling in a complex B2B context involves many different technical experts providing their expertise (eg the legal team, finance, product development, technology support) to help shape and/or deliver the solution. It takes many meetings to get all internal resources organised and aligned and to make sure everyone plays their critical part in the process. Often these internal meetings focus only on the technical ins and outs of the task (eg implementation advice, scoping and pricing for specific deliverables, time frames). At best, a bit of customer context is given by the salesperson to introduce the meeting.

Sharing the customer improvement goal can provide clarity and focus on the wider commercial context. It clarifies how the requested help or input from the different technical experts can support the broader customer objectives. Technical experts can craft a customer improvement opportunity as a commercial alignment tool if this has not been properly done for them, as we saw in the opportunities section of the COSMOS framework. Consistently articulating the customer improvement goal at the start of any activity or meeting will drive consistency and understanding of why actions are happening and, as a result, mobilise change more effectively.

Be a customer improvement broker throughout

The buying process for solutions can be long, and stakeholders within the customer organisation often change roles. It is likely that at the start of a sales cycle a specific customer challenge was identified and linked to the supplier's solution (products and/or services). As time goes by, however, and stakeholders change, the link between what has been sold and the impact it has on the customer's business challenges fades or gets lost in translation.

Someone has signed the contract in the past but new stakeholders do not necessarily know why the specific products and tools are implemented. To avoid weakening this link, everyone involved in the process of delivering solutions should be a messenger or broker of customer improvement. If the customer improvement goal is shared in a simple and transparent way, then it will remain clear, even if other project parameters and stakeholders change. It helps to ensure the link between the solution and the customer objectives does not weaken.

Technical experts who deliver (part of) a solution could use clear customer improvement statements to impact several buyer expectations at once. An important expectation is for you to demonstrate that you care about helping the customer's organisation become a better business.

REFLECTION: BUSINESS IMPACT AS PART OF TECHNICAL DELIVERY

Let's use a scenario to illustrate this. It usually takes several months to sign a deal in a complex B2B sales environment. Several months after the sale and the contractual paperwork have been completed, a technical expert could be resourced to perform a paid activity: scoping the necessary customisation of the solution or product.

The technical expert probably has tons of experience in all configuration possibilities. They are probably also even proficient at efficiently running this type of scoping workshop with different senior stakeholders. Here is what happens in most instances: the workshop is well prepared but seen as a purely technical intervention, and the technical expert dives straight into the mechanics of the task at hand. Is the technical expert seeing this workshop as a commercial opportunity? This will rarely be the case, but by using a simple customer improvement statement at the start of the session, everyone in that workshop can be reminded (in a non-sales setting) of how the supplier is aligned and focused to driving business impact within the client organisation.

The introduction could be as follows:

◎ **Your organisation is looking at reducing risk linked to staff turnover.**

⋀⋀ **We are able to predict where staff turnover is most likely to happen in the organisation and how to prevent this.**

✕ **The Employee Experience Management System we will configure today will help us set up the characteristics of people and teams in your organisation so that we will be able to offer relevant insight in our dashboard on how to best address flight risk in the specific parts of your organisation. Today's workshop will be focused on scoping the specifications to help us achieve those outcomes more effectively.**

How to deal with blockers

Blockers exist as a specific customer profile also high-lighted in the Challenger Customer research.[70] They may view new improvement projects as a distraction and therefore are not inclined to share useful information. Blockers cannot be ignored for two reasons: they will not disappear during the sales cycle, and they can seriously reduce the likelihood of a high-quality deal. Quickly identifying blockers will allow the creation of different messaging and engagement strategies to help minimise their impact and influence in the buying group.

The best way to neutralise blockers is to create com-mon ground and establish a process of collective learn-ing.[71] This can happen through facilitating a workshop in which different stakeholders can exchange views on the problem and solution. Collective learning can decrease the impact of blockers because it creates a larger group of supporters who can counteract them.

If the collective learning approach or social pressure approach do not work, the next tactic is to engage directly with the blocker to understand their motiva-tors. Why do they prefer not to change or change to a different provider or solution? Are they opposed to a certain supplier? Engaging directly with a blocker has a higher risk than going through the Mobilizer, because not everyone is keen to be confronted. It helps to diagnose the motivators for blocking and see how to find a solution to tackle these.

The last resort could be to involve the blocker's manager, but this should be used as your final escalation strategy only if none of the other techniques has worked. It always needs to be done with subtlety: using objective descriptions of the situation, motivators and blocking behaviours. Be careful: if the blocker feels pressured or takes it the wrong way, you may have created a bigger problem down the line.

Provide clear recommendations and an answer to 'Now what?'

As a technical expert, your role is to help a customer navigate alternatives, provide useful advice on the best course of action and help avoid potential risks. In doing so, you meet those buyer expectations that can lead to customer retention and growth.

Technical experts have the power to mobilise people by providing clear recommendations to drive action throughout the end-to-end sales and delivery process in the most desired direction. The temptation is to play it safe and always present all available options to the customer. A client question on what the best option or next steps would be is usually answered by: 'It depends.'

Although this is probably a true answer, customers want you to step into their shoes, understand their objectives and explain the rationale and assumptions you would use for what you see as the best course of action. Technical experts who provide clear recommendations and next steps will enable change to happen more quickly.

Many technical experts also have the opportunity to turn technical findings or data into insights, which means applying human judgement. Too often the focus is on the data rather than on the recommendations or the 'Now what?' question, which helps customers progress through their decision process and steer and mobilise change around your recommendations.

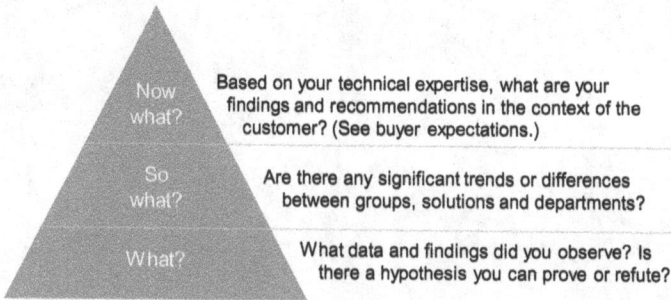

Based on your technical expertise, what are your findings and recommendations in the context of the customer? (See buyer expectations.)

Are there any significant trends or differences between groups, solutions and departments?

What data and findings did you observe? Is there a hypothesis you can prove or refute?

Mobilising change by answering the 'Now what?' question

To successfully mobilise people to join you on your journey, you need insight into your preferred communication style as well as that of the audience. This links back to how you can inspire someone and tailor the delivery to be persuasive enough for them to take action.

you would use for what you need, the best course of action. Technical experts who provide clear recommendations and next steps will enable change to happen more quickly.

Many technical experts also have the opportunity to turn technical findings or data into insights, which means applying human judgement. Too often the focus is on the data rather than on the customer; it distracts from the 'now what?' question, which helps customers progress through their decision process and steer and mobilise change around your recommendations.

Mobilising change by tone and the 'now what?' question

To successfully mobilise people to join you on your journey, you need insight into your preferred communication style as well as that of the audience. This links back to how you can mature someone and tailor the delivery to be persuasive enough for them to take action.

13
How Leaders Can Unlock The Commercial Potential Of Technical Experts

Every technical expert has unique needs and reasons that explain why they do (or do not) want to develop commercial capabilities. In many instances, the case for change still needs to be made or clarified. As with the development of many other workplace behaviours and skills, people leaders play a key role in helping their team members understand why it is important to learn specific skills which keep them relevant and employable. Leaders can also create an environment in which their team members will be fully committed to trying out new experiences and developing their expertise. Which leadership model should be adopted to help technical experts discover their commercial capabilities and increase the chances of successfully impacting customer improvement opportunities? What does it take for technical experts to perform at their best in their organisation?

In the next two chapters I will cover different best practices for people leaders to effectively unlock commercial potential of their technical experts. I will also offer tips on how to select, develop and manage technical experts and increase their commercial impact. Finally, I will cover the importance of technology and AI in understanding the needs of employees and predicting commercial impact at the individual, team or organisational level.

There is no one-size-fits-all leadership model

Sales and buying approaches have evolved significantly over the last two decades, and so have leadership models and approaches to drive employee and business performance. Every couple of years a new leadership model surfaces in the pursuit of increasing different people and organisational outcomes. According to Gartner in 2021, changing from one leadership model to another will, however, not drive better business outcomes, because there is no single model that turns out to be better than the others.[72]

The list below offers a snapshot of a few newer and more popular leadership models, highlighting the key takeaways from each and the reasons why these matter in the context of unlocking technical experts' commercial potential.[73,74,75,76]

Avocado leadership

Definition: Leaders have a soft, empathetic outer layer balanced with a harder, commercially focused core.

Inception: 2020

Key takeaway to help unlock commercial potential: Human focus

Benefits: Employees are increasingly looking to their employer to help meet their 'me' needs (physical, financial, employment, emotional/mental), their 'me and you' needs (relational) and their collective 'we' needs (purpose). By meeting these six fundamental human needs through the work environment, companies can unlock people's full potential.

Enterprise leadership

Definition: The whole is greater than the sum of its parts – which includes individuals, teams and business units in an organisation. Leaders ensure that every employee sees their contribution not just as achieving their individual tasks and objectives but also as enabling and leveraging the contributions of others to have an impact and add value.

Inception: 2014

Key takeaway to help unlock commercial potential: Organisational focus

Benefits: For technical experts, making a commercial impact will in most instances go beyond achieving what is outlined in traditional job descriptions. By ensuring technical experts focus on their expertise and individual tasks but also look for opportunities to add value and have a commercial impact on the broader enterprise, leaders can help to break a silo mentality around commercial impact, which is key to success.

Agile leadership

Definition: Leaders create the right context for self-organisation in ambiguous circumstances. They create an environment where teams collaborate, learn from each other, get quick feedback and are focused on quality and continual learning.

Inception: 2006

Key takeaway to help unlock commercial potential: Context focus

Benefits: The business and external environment in which organisations operate will continue to change. Understanding what a specific context requires to help technical experts become more commercially minded is more helpful than focusing on a one-size-fits-all approach across situations.

Digital leadership

Definition: Leaders use digital assets in a strategic way to achieve business goals. They also recognise that digital transformation is not about technology alone but about strategy, structure, culture, capabilities and a good understanding of the customer. Technology is a tool to be used rather than the end game.

Inception: 2002

Key takeaway to help unlock commercial potential: Customer and employee focus using digital assets

Benefits: Helping technical experts drive commercial impact will require an approach which keeps the concept of customer improvement at the centre. In a world after a global pandemic, we know that digital transformation is here to stay, and tools to support virtual communication and the creation of customer improvement insight will be critical to success. Technology can also be used to better understand the needs of employees and remove barriers which stand in the way of unlocking commercial potential.

Authentic leadership

Definition: Leaders are aware of the need to build positive relationships and inspire and encourage employees in the right ways.

Inception: 2001

Key takeaway to help unlock commercial potential: Honest focus

Benefits: By being honest and self-aware about which types of context and skill sets are most aligned to their leadership approach, leaders can look to establish connections with people who complement the missing leadership skills and provide effective and tailored commercial development to technical experts.

While all leadership models include core skills that leaders use in all contexts, pinpointing a set of skills that is useful in every situation is difficult. The broader external and internal business contexts (sales and buying) and the macroeconomic, social and environmental environments always have and always will change.

The future of work – in which commercial skills are embedded in the broader workforce – is not a fluffy, far-reaching concept, and leaders will have to balance **human, digital, customer, organisational** and **context needs** to help unlock the commercial potential of their team members. None of the different focus areas in isolation will be sufficient to develop commercial focus and/or successfully drive towards the outcomes. It is also unrealistic for leaders to be perfect in all these areas, and, therefore, **self-awareness** and **honesty** will be key to leading teams with authenticity. To unlock the full potential of technical experts, leaders should look for people to complement their existing teams and close the gaps, to help compensate for their own limitations.

Interestingly, as a leader you do not have to be better than your team members in all areas. Compare it to sports, where a good coach does not need to be as skilled in the sport as the players they lead. A good leader understands how to get the best out of every individual by connecting people to the right resources and learning partners (people who may have complementing skills) and by creating an environment in which employees can thrive and unlock their potential. Last but not least, in this time and age it is unthinkable that we are not looking at technology and science to help perform this critical task. I will cover the role of technology in better understanding the needs of employees to unlock their potential later in this part of the book.

Don't be blindsided by commercial experience

As a people leader, you may be in a position to hire new team members who can complement your team's capability with the missing technical expertise. Selecting the right individuals helps you to positively impact business strategy results, customer outcomes and investor and financial outcomes.[77] To ensure people stay employable in a workplace that continues to change and be more digital and automated, the hiring focus should be not only on what is needed today (eg specific technical expertise) but also on what is needed for the future.

Ideally, the technical experts joining your team should (in addition to their technical skills) have the potential to use uniquely human skills such as critical thinking, collaboration, learning and adapting, and be resilient to ever-changing work requirements. The inclination of employees to engage in self-directed learning and their desire to maximise their commercial potential will also be important if your organisation wants to stay aligned to future workforce needs. As highlighted in the first chapter, having a commercially minded and skilled workforce is essential for organisations to be successful in the twenty-first century, especially in a complex B2B environment.

Does this mean you should select only technical experts who have commercial experience listed on their CV? Past commercial experience is not necessarily indicative of future success or performance in a new work environment. As part of the selection process, a recruiter or people leader needs to look for commercial potential.

The commercial AIM and the COSMOS framework can be adopted without commercial experience. If technical experts have potential and there is a culture conducive to learning and development, they may be able to rapidly increase their impact.

REFLECTION: CHOOSING BEYOND PREVIOUS COMMERCIAL EXPERIENCE

A friend of mine once called me to get my opinion on a career opportunity. After more than a decade of working for the same company as a B2B salesperson, she had decided it was time for a change. Two new work opportunities surfaced for her to choose from.

The first was a 'hunter' sales role, which involved selling in a B2B context, predominantly working alone and from home. The work environment in her last role had been one of the reasons she wanted to change jobs: there was always tension between departments and individuals, which impacted the customer experience. Although it was tempting to choose this opportunity for an individual work setting and exclude most of the negative aspects of her previous role, that would have been a short-term fix because working with colleagues was more aligned to her working style preferences.

The second opportunity consisted of working in a local retail bank, selling retail banking products to customers (B2C sales). Based on her experience (which is what most traditional recruiters look at), the B2B sales role would have been the most logical move, but she also had the intellectual aptitude to understand more complex products and customer and organisational needs. She was motivated to learn new skills, products and processes and was energised by the fact she would work in a completely new context.

The more important question was which of those two job opportunities could inspire her to perform at her best and stay engaged for a longer period of time. The answer did not lie in her past commercial experience but in her commercial potential. She chose the B2C role and continues to be both happy and successful in her new role today.

Provide clarity on the best collaboration approach

To help technical experts feel comfortable in spotting and seizing commercial opportunities, there needs to be a culture in which this type of broader contribution is considered, accepted and supported. This does not mean a technical expert should expect to spend the majority of their time doing work they were not hired for in the first place. It means there is an openness to people broadening their role if this can help their company be more successful.

It is important not to leave everything open to interpretation: teamwork between sales team members and technical experts is needed. The reality is, however, that productive teamwork between sales and technical experts can be difficult to achieve.

Recent research on team collaboration concludes that maximising teamwork at all costs is less effective than rightsizing teamwork.[78] This requires a change in mindset but is the best way to achieve the agility and resilience that are needed to help drive different types of customer improvement opportunities. It is everyone's role in the organisation to help seize commercial opportunities when spotted, but not at all costs or when this leads to potential inefficiencies.

Teamwork as an optimised cross-functional practice between technical experts and salespeople rarely gets much attention, but leaders play a key role in creating seamless connections. As a leader, you can ask yourself: 'Who should be involved in which stage of the end-to-end sales and delivery process and in what capacity? Are the people involved in the team also responsible and accountable, or is it enough for them to be informed?'

Although a broader collaboration framework will be helpful for people to understand the overall expectations and responsibilities, it requires a deeper understanding of the commercial potential of each technical expert to make this work effectively. Some technical experts may be skilled at spotting new customer improvement opportunities (the context and opportunity parts of COSMOS); others may be better at understanding the stakeholders and motivators but less inclined to strategise and work out what needs to be done to move the plan forward towards completion in front of a customer. There is no universal best practice collaboration approach, but this is where commercial potential (personality preferences, motivation and intellectual aptitudes) should be aligned to the needs of the customer, the context and the organisation.

Create a growth culture

As a leader of technical experts, you are responsible for shaping a growth culture (instead of a performance-obsessed culture). This is a culture in which every activity is seen as an opportunity for learning and individuals can take ownership of their personal development and performance, and ongoing forward-looking performance conversations become the norm. This includes the development of commercial capability. Technical experts are often in a strong position to spot customer improvement opportunities, but they do not necessarily see it as their role or responsibility to sell the idea or drive towards the execution of the opportunity. As a leader of technical experts, you can start by setting clear expectations about the fact that thinking about customer improvement is expected from everyone in the team.

To help technical experts be more effective in driving customer improvement opportunities on an ongoing basis, part of a people leader's role needs to be managing their overall performance. There are three key strategies which drive employee performance in a given area:

1. You embrace ongoing conversations instead of talking about the performance of your technical expert only once or twice a year. Research confirms that ongoing performance conversations can lead to levels of engagement and retention of employees that are 1.5 times higher and can have a positive impact on employee performance by an average of 12%.[79] In my survey, unfortunately only 27% of respondents say this is the case.

In the organisations I have worked for, performance conversations between a manager and their direct reports happen on average: (sample size = 536)

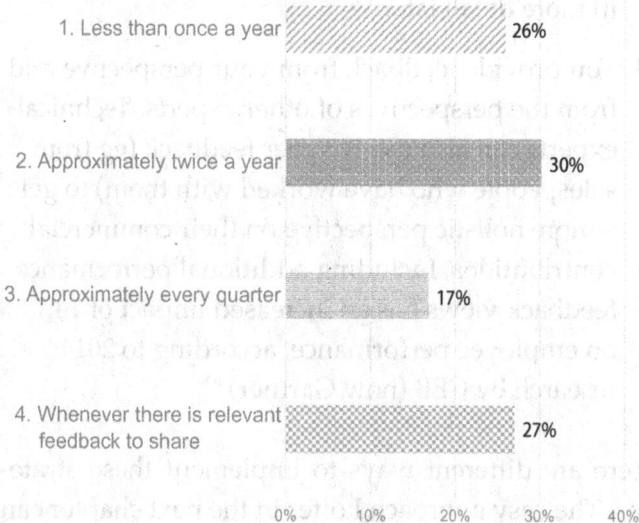

1. Less than once a year — 26%

2. Approximately twice a year — 30%

3. Approximately every quarter — 17%

4. Whenever there is relevant feedback to share — 27%

0%   10%   20%   30%   40%

Frequency of performance conversations between technical experts and their managers[80]

2. You don't dwell on the past but embed more forward-looking performance reviews into your practice, given that, according to 2012 research by CEB (now Gartner), this positively impacts employee performance by an average of 13%.[81] In my survey, 67% of respondents state that their manager does focus the performance conversation on what's possible in the future. This is a good start, but do managers know what to focus on in the future and how to increase commercial impact? Have they considered which aspects could be boosting or blocking commercial development at individual, team or organisational level? We will dive into this topic in more detail later.

3. You provide feedback from your perspective and from the perspectives of other experts. Technical experts can also receive peer feedback (eg from salespeople who have worked with them) to get a more holistic perspective on their commercial contributions. Including additional performance feedback views has an increased impact of 14% on employee performance, according to 2014 research by CEB (now Gartner).[82]

There are different ways to implement these strategies. The easy approach I offer in the next chapter can be used immediately by every people leader alongside any formal performance management strategy which may have been mandated centrally in the organisation.

14
Stimulating Self-insight And Ownership Of Development

In this chapter we will look at different ways to increase self-awareness and unlock commercial potential in people and organisations using a conversation framework and reflection questions for employees and people managers. We will explore the role and links of psychometrics (personality, values and employee experience) in relation to COSMOS and AIM and the development of commercial capabilities. If technical experts and leaders want to look for customer improvement opportunities to bridge different functional or organisational cultures, then we need to review how we select, develop and reward customer improvement brokers. Finally, we will explore the use of technology and AI for understanding people and teams and making the preparation of customer improvement opportunities more impactful and effective.

Customer improvement reflection circle

The **customer improvement reflection circle** below can be embedded into all day-to-day work activities and routines and offers an easy framework to reflect on past contributions and future opportunities. Customer improvement, as described in previous chapters, drives towards positive commercial outcomes and should sit at the core of everyone's mindset and behaviours.

Every technical expert working for you can reflect on these four questions. The circle can be used for performance and development conversations between employee and manager. It will help in discussions to balance what has happened in the past with what is possible in the future. When discussing performance, the focus usually lies predominantly on the past. More energy and reflection should be spent on improving the future and driving new, different or better customer improvement opportunities.

Customer improvement reflection circle

Reflecting on performance or impact in the past

'What customer improvement DID I achieve?'

This is a simple question which should prompt a review on the customer improvement contributions you made and how you went about achieving impact. Taking time to reflect on how you did this will help you increase the effectiveness of your future contributions. Past performance does not predict future performance, so if as a technical expert you have nothing specific to answer yet to this question, this means you

CUSTOMER IMPROVEMENT SELLING

have an opportunity to take control of what can happen in the future. Using the behavioural AIM outcomes will help to drive commercial impact and help you focus on how you can take your ongoing commercial development into your own hands.

'What customer improvement DID **we** achieve?'

Thinking about the broader organisation and adding value beyond your own technical impact will open new perspectives and help customers and the organisation move forward in a more effective way. It helps to think across silos and see how the sum of the parts can contribute to something bigger. Contributions outside of your formal role towards the success of the organisation can sometimes go unrecognised, but it is important to reflect on and understand what the learnings and outcomes have been so you can bottle, repeat or scale these where appropriate.

Reflecting on future potential

'What customer improvement CAN **I** achieve?'

Shaping customer improvement opportunities starts with an intent to drive your behaviour in a different or more effective way. Your behaviours are driven by your potential (eg working style preferences, motivation and value drivers, and capacity to deal with connected topics) and also by your existing capabilities,

which can include technical knowledge and skills (the knowledge and application of frameworks and best practices proven to lead to commercial outcomes) and your experience – for example, did you learn in a relevant comparable context or in a situation which made you act in a different way?

'What customer improvement CAN **we** achieve?'

As a technical expert you are likely to have a different and valuable perspective on what could be done differently to drive customer improvement opportunities, even outside of your individual impact. Regularly reflecting on what these aspirations could look like and discussing the different perspectives on this topic helps to create an agile environment which makes the processes and people more aligned to new or changing customer needs in a team, organisation or even, more broadly, in the industry you operate in.

You can use the same four questions to offer your perspectives to the technical expert you are managing, or by involving different peer perspectives and feedback. As a manager of a technical expert, you would change the 'I' to 'my direct report' in the questions presented in the Customer Improvement Reflection Circle.

Coaching is another great skill for leaders to develop further. Many organisations consider this as a core skill in leadership development programmes. Coaching

is about creating a trusting environment where people can learn from mistakes and are encouraged to reflect. It is about helping your team members obtain self-insight and take ownership of finding solutions to problems. It is important to enable connections across silos for people to learn from their peers in other teams. As a leader, you need to broker peer and team connections as well as coaching opportunities which scale the learning and have great organisational impact.

Can personality and value assessments help?

We know leaders and HR professionals are relatively familiar with using predictive psychometric assessment tools in a selection context. When using these tools, the focus is on understanding the now and the immediate impact someone can have in a new role. Commercial potential for technical experts is likely not considered to make selection decisions.

Self-insight is key to helping people take ownership of their professional development and careers. It gives them the opportunity to steer in a direction where they can shine or look for help from others to compensate for areas of development.

Psychometric assessments are typically used by HR teams to make selection decisions in a more objective way. They can also be part of leadership development

programmes to offer leaders more self-insight. People in non-leadership roles should also be offered the opportunity to complete predictive psychometric assessments to help improve self-insight and understand in more detail their strengths and areas for development to drive commercial impact in a given context.

My international study of technical experts included a personality and a value framework. The personality questionnaire which I used with the international sample was developed in line with the European Federation of Psychologists' Associations standards. It is designed around the well-established 'Big Five' model of personality and consists of the following five dimensions:[83,84]

- Learning and change mindset (openness to experience)

- Goal and delivery focus (conscientiousness)

- Group impact (extraversion)

- Interpersonal impact (agreeableness)

- Emotional self-management (emotional stability)

The model is broken down into thirty different scales as per the figure below. Every individual who completes the short survey receives a normed score (1–9) on the five different factors (eg group impact) with a short description of what this means in terms of the potential positive or negative impact of this score on the individual.

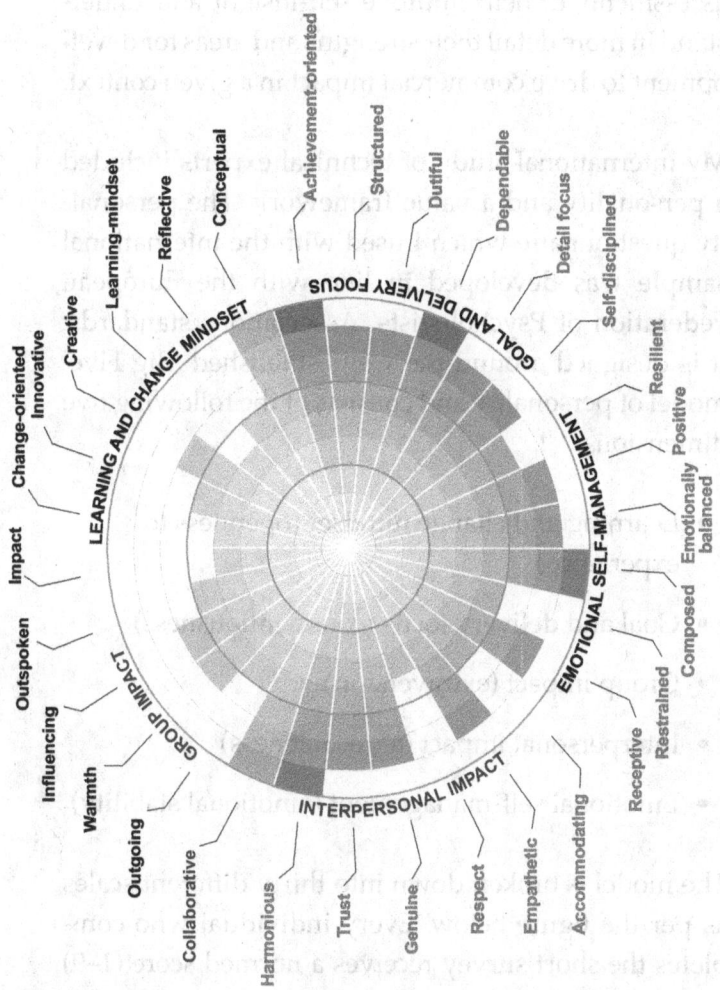

GOAL AND DELIVERY FOCUS

Achievement-oriented
Structured
Dutiful
Dependable
Detail focus
Self-disciplined

Conceptual
Reflective
Learning-mindset

LEARNING AND CHANGE MINDSET

Creative
Innovative
Change-oriented

Impact

GROUP IMPACT

Outspoken
Influencing
Warmth
Outgoing
Collaborative

INTERPERSONAL IMPACT

Harmonious
Trust
Genuine
Respect
Empathetic
Accommodating

EMOTIONAL SELF-MANAGEMENT

Receptive
Restrained
Composed
Emotionally balanced
Positive
Resilient

An example of a random individual personality profile[85]

The table below shows which of the personality traits support the key AIM behaviours. People have spiky personality profiles; you cannot find a person who will likely score highly on all these dimensions. Understanding the strengths and development opportunities someone has will help leaders to see where support is needed to maximise their contributions. As we discussed earlier, preferred behaviour doesn't mean it will always translate into actual behaviour. Specific aspects in someone's environment can boost or block certain behaviours.

Technical experts who are effective at mobilising change have a tendency to be reflective and receptive. They are likely to be open to receiving advice and criticism, proactively encouraging others to share their feedback and understanding what can be done differently to increase the chances of a desired outcome. This approach will likely help focus on areas where review and change tactics are needed to drive customer improvement opportunities forward. In addition to this, if people combine a positive attitude with a focus on innovation, they will likely create more impact and understanding about what may hinder or help progress with different stakeholders to advance customer improvement ideas. With their achievement orientation, they are looking for ways to get the support of other Mobilizers and reduce the negative impact of blockers on implementing customer improvement ideas. As we have seen, people leaders play a key role in supporting a growth mindset and a culture of ongoing feedback. By also providing a

Link between AIM and thirteen personality traits

Understanding of key areas of AIM	Statistically significant correlations of personality traits to the separate AIM behavious (traits in bold have a high correlation to all AIM behaviours)[84]
Anticipate needs: Understanding what's needed to shape and plan customer improvement	• Change-oriented • **Conceptual** • **Influential** • Impactful • Outspoken • Positive
Inspire with insight: Influencing customer improvement by using effective communication techniques (eg reframing, questions) and aligning to different communication styles	• **Conceptual** • **Influential** • **Impactful** • **Outspoken**
Mobilise change: Enabling progress towards customer improvement by driving collective learning and consensus in decision-making and approach	• Reflective • Innovative • **Conceptual** • Achievement-oriented • Self-disciplined • **Influential** • **Impactful** • **Outspoken** • Harmonious • Receptive • Positive • Resilient

framework for reflection opportunities which lead to driving the behaviours that are more likely to increase commercial outcomes, the chances are that more commercial potential can be unlocked in the team if managers and the broader organisation collectively change to this approach.

Which personality traits can support commercial impact and help think through the relevant questions as per the COSMOS preparation framework? We can also find statistical linkages to specific personality traits here, as shown in the table below.

Link between COSMOS and eight personality traits

Understanding of key areas of COSMOS	Statistically significant correlations of personality traits to the separate COSMOS dimensions (traits in bold have a high correlation to all COSMOS dimensions)[87]
Context: Having an understanding of what happens in the world of the customer and how this links to business strategy, revenue and growth	• Reflective • **Conceptual** • Achievement-oriented • **Influential** • Impactful • Harmonious • Receptive

Understanding of key areas of COSMOS	Statistically significant correlations of personality traits to the separate COSMOS dimensions (traits in bold have a high correlation to all COSMOS dimensions)[87]
Opportunity: Ability to identify customer improvement opportunities and to communicate about them	• Reflective • **Conceptual** • Achievement-oriented • **Influential** • Impactful • Harmonious • Positive
Stakeholders: Ability to find relevant stakeholders, understand their priorities and identify who will (not) care about customer improvement	• **Conceptual** • **Influential** • Impactful
Motivation: Ability to understand what motivates (no) change	• Reflective • **Conceptual** • **Influential** • Impactful
Objections: Ability to anticipate obstacles and identify areas to make the change journey easier	• Reflective • **Conceptual** • **Influential**
Strategy: Ability to plan and act towards realising commercial outcomes	• **Conceptual** • **Influential** • Impactful

Values influence the way people behave. There are nineteen basic, motivationally distinct values that people in virtually all cultures implicitly recognise. Schwartz's values framework is a well-established model with a significant body of research to support it. It offers a picture of primary concerns, drivers and cultural context within which people can help achieve their potential. Studies were conducted on a range of international samples. Most notable is a large study published in 2021, providing reliability and validity evidence for the latest version of the values questionnaire across forty-nine cultural groups and thirty-two language versions with a sample of over 50,000 participants.[88]

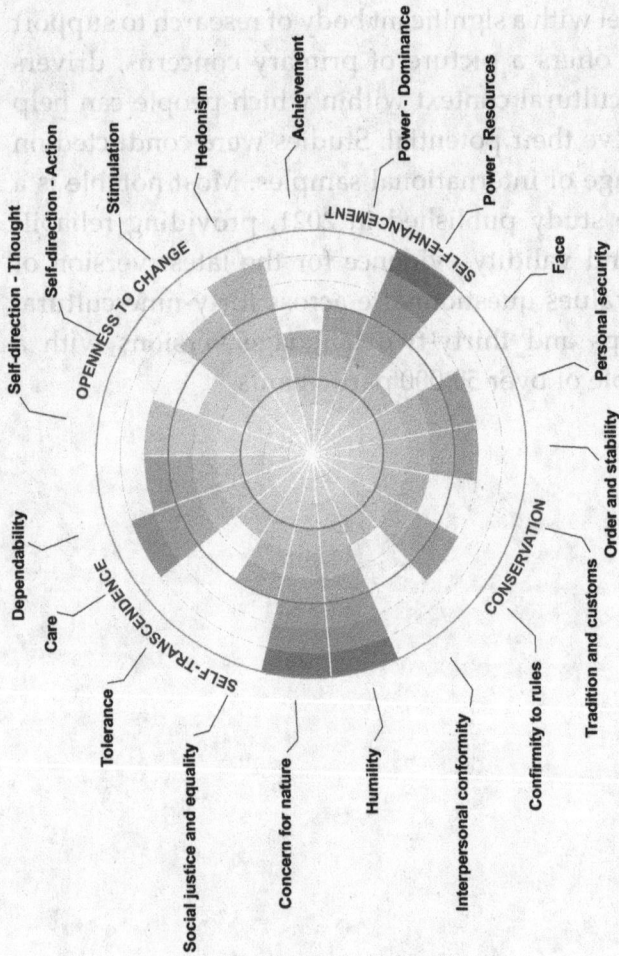

An example of a value profile for one individual[89]

For more detailed information about the meaning of the dimensions please refer to the appendix. The below table shows which values correlate with the AIM behaviours.

Strong statistical links between AIM and individual values

	Statistically significant correlations of individual values that map against specific AIM behaviours (values in bold map to all AIM behaviours)[90]
Anticipate needs: understanding what's needed to shape and plan customer improvement	Achievement
Inspire with insight: influencing customer improvement by using effective communication techniques (eg reframing, questions) and aligning to different communication styles	Stimulation **Achievement**
Mobilise change: enabling progress towards customer improvement by driving collective learning and consensus in decision-making and approach	Achievement Independent thought Concern for nature

The individual value of 'achievement' correlates with all of the AIM behaviours. This means that people who score highly on this value are likely to be ambitious and driven to succeed. They take delight in being recognised for their achievements. People with a high score on achievement tend to score themselves highly for rallying others behind a new improvement idea, looking at ways to be effective at implementing new ideas and thinking that the organisation can help them realise their own potential and capabilities. These behavioural attributes in combination with the value 'concern for nature' will be a great driver for organisations, as this is critical for customer improvement opportunities which will lead organisations and society to sustainable growth.

Select, develop and reward customer improvement brokers

Earlier in the book, we explored the idea of a cultural broker: an individual who facilitates interactions between people who have different sets of assumptions, values and norms based on cross-silo leadership research from Casciaro, AC Edmondson and S Jang.[91] If technical experts want to look for customer improvement opportunities which bridge different functional or organisational cultures, it is important for leaders to facilitate this type of collaboration. A narrow focus on immediate functional goals is often standing in the way of enabling and seizing new customer improvement opportunities. When respondents in my survey were asked the reason for not being able to convince people of the relevance of their customer improvement ideas, their responses showed that line managers do not believe this is something these individuals need to be focused on. Customer improvement ideas can't be implemented, because people and functional teams work on their own priorities and most approaches to customer improvement need cross-function collaboration.[92]

Using the questions in the customer improvement reflection circle can help to detect potential openness to seeing more widely than the individual focus, as the answers to the 'we' questions will provide insight into broader perspectives, appetite and the ability to connect dots which may not be seen by everyone. It also takes resilience to work with people across functional divides, and leaders should look for a growth mindset – the desire to learn from setbacks or not achieving immediate wins.

In addition, leaders can develop more brokers by giving people at all levels the chance to move into roles that expose them to multiple parts of the company. Sometimes a short-term project, or 'stretch' opportunity, can help to deepen connections and broaden perspectives. Short rotational leadership programmes aim to accomplish this but, unfortunately, they are available only to the select few.

The importance of understanding employee experience

The term 'employee experience' (EX) is often explained as an analogy to 'customer experience' (CX), which is defined as 'the relationship that a customer has with a brand'.[93] The relationship between employees and their organisation is more complex than the relationship between a customer and a brand, but, in the same way as a positive customer experience can lead to better business outcomes, achieving a great employee experience is critical to realising better business and people outcomes. According to a recent study, the outcomes of a positive EX are better workforce and organisational agility, better innovation, improved attraction and retention of talent, higher productivity and higher-quality work, increased revenue, profitability and growth, better brand reputation and better customer satisfaction.[94]

How can we define a positive employee experience for technical experts in the organisation? Is the organisational environment conducive to technical experts contributing to customer improvement ideas and opportunities?

It is important to understand what a positive EX looks like, because this makes it possible to define a goal that can be worked towards. The goal is to have the best possible overlap of expectations and needs that can support developing commercial capability in technical experts on the one hand, and the tools and approaches designed by the organisation to align to those expectations and needs on the other. Ultimately, organisations need to help technical experts unlock their commercial potential and increase their impact on organisational success.

EX practices today are mostly immature. There is a disconnect between what leaders think is happening in the workplace and what is perceived by employees. Leaders and HR certainly care and are investing in ways to listen and collect input on employees' needs. They tend to rely on surveys, interviews and/or focus groups to listen, but feedback from employees is often inconsistent and difficult to analyse and integrate across silos (eg sales, learning and development, and technical departments).

Current EX approaches mostly overlook people's potential and their personal characteristics. Instead, they tend to focus on areas that are linked to the environment of the individual. As we have seen, there are specific individual values and personality traits that can lead to better customer improvement outcomes, but we need to understand the needs and experiences of technical experts in their unique context.

Welliba® is an international company that specialises in EX insight and management. I joined Welliba in 2021. After analysing the shortcomings of current models, Welliba's behavioural scientists designed and launched a new model for EX. The new model was based on extensive research of scientific publications about EX and related scientific fields. They defined EX as 'the subjective experience of how employees perceive their life and work and the organisation they work in'. These perceptions result from the interaction between the employee's characteristics (personality, mindset, ability, attitudes, values, needs and motivation) and external factors in the environment.[95]

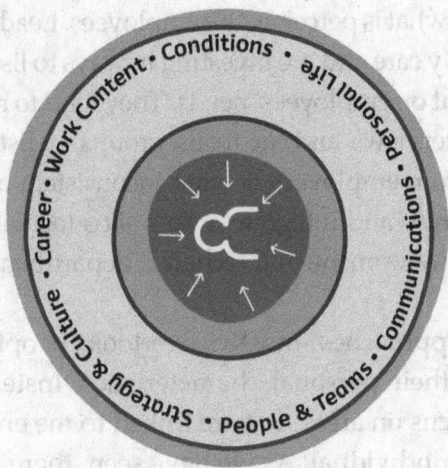

Context Insight

Strategy & Culture · People & Teams · Communications · Personal Life · Conditions · Work Content · Career

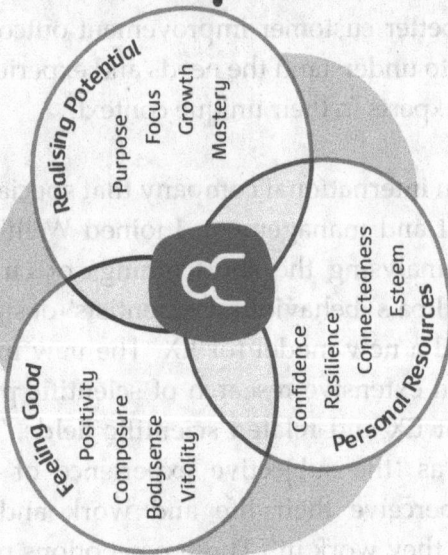

Self-Insight

Realising Potential
- Purpose
- Focus
- Growth
- Mastery

Feeling Good
- Positivity
- Composure
- Bodysense
- Vitality

Personal Resources
- Confidence
- Resilience
- Connectedness
- Esteem

Welliba's Employee Experience Index

Employee experience: a dynamic interaction between a person (self) and their environment (context)

Of all respondents in my research study, 44% state that their commercial potential is underused. This leads to a critical question: what may be holding technical experts back in trying to unlock more of their commercial potential and drive greater impact in the organisation? To find this out, organisations and managers need to capture predictive and relevant insights directly from their employees. Using a validated and scientific model of employee experience that links specific EX dimensions to improved business, people and innovation outcomes is an effective way to drive change towards higher use of commercial potential in the organisation.

In the study, technical experts also completed a short employee experience survey based on the scientific and validated EX model of Welliba described above. I will summarise some of the highest statistical correlations between the dimensions from this EX model and their relationship to direct outcome statements provided by the respondents.[96,97]

Self-insight

Technical experts who have a high score on **feeling supported** (**connectedness** in personal resources) tend to have a direct manager who is supportive not just of their commercial development but also of their overall development and wellbeing. They also feel supported by their organisation because there is an openness to new customer improvement ideas and overall employee development. A culture of supportive organisational development is likely to fuel innovation and learning which technical experts agree provides them with valuable feedback on how to increase their commercial impact.

Respondents with a high **optimistic** score (**confidence** in personal resources) tend to see their managers as being supportive of commercial and broader development. They would also agree that there is a general openness in the organisation to working on customer improvement ideas and that sales and technical teams have similar priorities on how to achieve joint customer outcomes. At the beginning of the book, we identified that a lack of alignment between the goals of technical teams and sales can be a key factor in limiting the development of commercial capability in technical experts.

People who perceive high **purpose** (realising potential) – which means they feel that their job is fulfilling and meaningful, so worth investing effort in – tend to have managers who are supportive of their commercial development and care about their wellbeing. They view their organisation as being open to working on customer improvement ideas. They feel sales and technical expert teams have similar priorities on how to achieve joint customer outcomes. The relationships between the outcome statements and perceived purpose are similar to those of technical experts scoring high on connectedness.

Technical experts with a high **career** score (**growth in realising potential**) see themselves as being effective at implementing new ideas in the organisation. It is no surprise that these people feel connected to the company's commercial strategy and corporate goals. They perceive strong manager support on commercial capability and broader development, and the development and effectiveness of their commercial capability is likely linked to having colleagues who are part of their learning journey and offer feedback to increase their commercial impact.

Context insight

Technical experts with a positive **work environment** score (**conditions**) and strong **values** alignment (**strategy and culture**) perceive support from their manager to develop their commercial capability. They also perceive an openness in the organisation to working on customer improvement ideas and overall employee development. The managers of these technical experts conduct future-focused performance conversations and care about the employees' broader development and wellbeing. Their colleagues play a role in offering feedback on what can be improved or changed to increase commercial impact. There is a perceived connection to the company's commercial strategy, corporate goals and priorities to achieve joint customer outcomes. This is similar between sales and technical teams.

As expected, there is also a clear link between **corporate communications** and a better understanding of one's individual commercial potential and capabilities. Positive perceptions of corporate communications are associated with opportunities for the development of commercial capabilities as well as alignment with corporate strategy and goals. This can help to create an environment in which it is easier for managers to facilitate a culture of constructive feedback to help increase commercial impact and support the organisational philosophy of learning and development.

In a market that has a shortage of skilled talent, and especially commercial talent, we need to consider that several of these dimensions of strong employee experience can directly impact employee retention. A better understanding of these drivers in the team or the organisation can reduce the 'flight risk' of valuable and scarce talent. In an international EX outcome study, Welliba defined flight risk as the likelihood that an employee intends to leave their job within the next six months.[98] Considering the range of possible negative effects on businesses, such as loss of technical expertise and costs associated with hiring and replacements, early recognition of increasing flight risk is crucial.

For flight risk, the most predictive drivers of Welliba's EX model are **purpose** (sees job as meaningful, fulfilling and worth investing effort in), **focus** (on goals and how to achieve them), **connected-ness** (maintains long-lasting relationships at work and feels supported by others), **team dynamics and culture**, **direct manager** and **top-down communication** (senior leadership to employees). This is based on their high negative correlations (if one variable increases, the other decreases), as shown in the table below.

Correlations of the person and context factors with 'Intention to quit within the next six months'[99]

	The values of a linear negative correlation range from 0 to -1
Purpose	-.54***
Focus	-.44***
Connectedness	-.35***
Team dynamics and culture	-.38***
Direct manager	-.39***
Top-down communication	-.35***

Note: *** indicates $p < 0.001$

Many of the key ingredients for technical experts to be successful in developing their commercial capability depend on perceived and appropriate manager support. Calculated and expressed from the statistical analysis in a different way: technical experts who are supported by their manager feel 9.5 times more able to grow in their career. If the manager support is missing, only 9.2% of people feel able to grow their commercial capability and career. In a market where there is a shortage of commercial talent, this is a critical aspect to take into consideration to retain talented individuals who may be able to drive commercial outcomes.

As we have seen, there is no one-size-fits-all approach to appropriate manager support. We need to understand the individual needs and scientific drivers of EX and the exact boosters and blockers of technical experts' learning and development. Technical experts need to be allowed to develop self-insight so that they don't need to wait for anyone to start unlocking their commercial potential. By understanding the needs of technical experts at scale in the organisation, leaders and central teams such as sales enablement and HR can share ownership in creating a culture and organisation in which people can unlock their commercial potential.

The use of technology

How can technology help to focus the resources and development investments in people and/or their environment so that they can make a real difference when it comes to people and business outcomes? Technology has taken a prominent role in many organisational departments. Sales and marketing teams use survey technology to keep track of the customer voice and experience with the company's products and customer services teams. Dashboards help to find trends and improvements in customer services and products. Learning and development teams support the ongoing development and needs of people in the organisation, again based on traditional approaches to capturing training needs, employee satisfaction and engagement.

In 2021, research conducted by Willis Towers Watson revealed that nine out of ten employers consider EX to be a top priority for their organisation, with 92% of employers reporting that managing and enhancing EX will be at the top of their HR agenda for the next three years.[100] The results revealed that only one in ten employers had integrated EX and business strategies and used technology to transform EX. Employee experience is critical to improving business outcomes, but a myriad of immature approaches and technologies are used to make sense of the needs of employees at different times in their careers. In recent years, many companies have been increasing their HR tech solutions in the form of new platforms to listen to and understand employees. A variety of technical and soft skills courses are offered via learning management systems and learning experience systems. There is an urgent need for a modernised, innovative approach to EX management that provides rich and informative data while simultaneously ensuring a high level of employee confidentiality. If we want to unlock the commercial potential of technical experts, we need to go beyond current approaches to employee listening and needs analysis, which leave central teams and managers with low-quality and often out-of-date data on trends or challenges blocking people development. Most surveys on employee listening or technologies to understand what people need to grow their potential are flawed on many fronts. They do not always offer predictive real-time and actionable insight for the organisation and managers to improve the situation. Data is not handled confidentially, which leads to incomplete and irrelevant aggregate feedback.

The main flaw of current EX technologies is that employees do not get personalised insight and guidance on what they can do to develop and improve their EX. No employee has ever learned from a survey how to drive new customer improvement opportunities and behaviours going forward. We cannot assume that employees know where to start or how to seize their individual potential. People come to work with a purpose: they want to feel connected and inspired around the commercial strategy and company goals and get a clear understanding on what they can do to increase their impact. Which specific blockers are preventing personal and business growth? Which hidden opportunities linked to the individual's characteristics or environment could lead to increased commercial impact? As business leaders, we need to look across the silos. Can we look for trends and drivers of a better EX for technical experts across the different customer groups (internal and external), teams and functions? Where do we see pockets of behaviours and ideas that can lead to more customer improvement best practices?

It was not until recently that behavioural science was coupled with human-centred technology to understand the dynamic interaction between people and their environment. This new combination has made it possible to offer scalable insight to individuals, managers and the central teams into the aspects that can help unlock commercial potential. Suddenly, new questions start surfacing and opportunities to take action arise. Organisations that use technology to anticipate, predict and quickly respond to their employees' and customers' needs are able to improve revenue growth potential.[101] It is only when business leaders and technical experts are equipped with a better understanding of the links between their technical world and the buying universe that they will be able to effectively impact customer improvement opportunities.

The new possibilities of AI

AI applications can now reduce the amount of time that sales teams and technical experts need to spend on finding information for the COSMOS preparation checklist. AI can be used to prompt and gather insights about the environment in which a company operates, or explore the pain points of different stakeholders and organisations which lead to competitive weaknesses or customer improvement opportunities. AI can also support sales and technical experts who need inspiration to craft a customer improvement message.

As highlighted, in order to unlock commercial potential in an organisation, we need to discover where key employee experience boosters and blockers are that prevent learning and productivity. AI can also help organisations understand what needs to happen in their supplier organisations to close gaps that separate them from industry or best in class organisations.

AI can efficiently combine existing data from multiple sources. Passive data is data previously generated or shared. This kind of data exists both outside of an organisation in the public domain, and internally within a company, potentially captured in separate technology platforms. Interestingly, lots of information about organisations is created by current and former employees. Imagine combining data from social media posts employer review boards and analyst reports with the internal data you already have, such as psychometrics assessments, exit interviews, absence rates and customer satisfaction ratings. By combining a validated model of employee experience with several AI applications, organisations can now unveil new perspectives linked to proven EX drivers of commercial capability development in a matter of hours. Such an approach would be a valuable complement to the specifically generated internal data gained from survey technologies.

Conclusion

Although many leaders in organisations may believe the research that states that strong employee experience, engagement and wellbeing drive better customer and business outcomes, they do not necessarily act on it. It is like rationally understanding the case for change but not seeing the emotional connection or feeling the urgency to do something about it.

I began this book by saying that 51% of respondents in my survey state: 'If I had a better understanding of how I could drive and support commercial outcomes, I would have a bigger impact in my organisation.' I hope that the book has helped its readers to get a better understanding of the potential keys to success but, more importantly, that it has given readers insights that can motivate them to initiate change. There is still a considerable distance between the starting point, where we are now and the destination, where the capabilities of technical experts are fully used to improve commercial impact. Silo walls can be intimidating, and people and organisations do not change overnight. A successful way for technical experts to start the change process would be to look for (other) change agents who can help drive change across their organisation.

In the book, we have often looked at how to close great sales deals and create client loyalty, which is fundamental to keeping business financially viable, but there is even more at stake. As the pressure mounts to find more sustainable ways of doing business, I hope those who are concerned by environmental issues will find different ways to unlock customer improvement potential and have their voices heard as they help organisations choose new directions towards a sustainable future.

Are you inspired?

Appendices

I conducted international research with 536 employees who were not currently working in a sales role. The respondents spanned twelve countries and a variety of industries, roles, gender and age groups. The tables below provide the percentages against different demographic characteristics of this research sample.

Research sample details

Country distribution (n=536)

	Female	Male	Prefer not to say
Australia	3.17%	3.36%	
Belgium	3.17%	3.36%	

Chile	2.43%	1.31%	
France	2.43%	4.10%	
Germany	2.80%	3.36%	
Hong Kong SAR, China	2.99%	1.87%	
Netherlands	3.36%	2.24%	
Singapore	3.54%	2.99%	
South Africa	1.68%	2.80%	
Spain	2.80%	3.73%	
United Kingdom	19.03%	18.47%	0.19%
United States	1.87%	2.99%	

Age (n=536)

1943–1957 (65+)	10.90%
1958–1967 (55–64)	29.70%
1968–1977 (45–54)	23.13%
1978–1987 (35–44)	18.47%
1988–1997 (25–34)	16.95%
1998–2007 (18–24)	0.95%

Job sector (n=536)

Agriculture	0.56%
Banking	1.68%
Construction	5.78%
Consulting	4.29%
Education	10.26%
Energy	0.93%
Engineering	1.68%

Finance	5.97%
Government	8.96%
Healthcare	11.01%
Hospitality	2.80%
Manufacturing	8.40%
Not for profit	2.43%
Retail	8.02%
Technology	6.72%
Telecommunications	1.87%
Other	17.16%
Prefer not to answer	1.49%

Job role (n=536)

Analytics and data science	2.05%
Digital marketing	0.37%
Education and training	7.65%
Engineering	4.10%
Executive / General management	8.40%
Finance and accounting	8.21%
General and administrative support	11.01%
Healthcare	7.47%
Hospitality and tourism	2.05%
Human resources	3.36%
Information technology	9.89%
Legal and compliance	1.12%
Marketing	0.75%

Operations	8.77%
Project and programme management	2.24%
Property management and construction	2.05%
Research and development	1.49%
Retail	4.85%
Strategy and policy creation and implementation	0.19%
Unemployed	0.19%
Other	12.87%
Prefer not to answer	0.93%

Value factors and scales used in Valpeo's Values Orientation Survey based on original human values research of Prof Schwartz[102]

Factor	Scales
Openness to change	• Self-direction – Thought
	• Self-direction – Action
	• Stimulation
	• Hedonism
Self-enhancement	• Achievement
	• Power – Dominance
	• Power – Resources
	• Face

Conservation	• Personal security
	• Order and stability
	• Tradition and customs
	• Conformity to rules
	• Interpersonal conformity
	• Humility
Self-transcendence	• Concern for nature
	• Social justice and equality
	• Tolerance
	• Care
	• Dependability

Definitions of high scores for values used in Valpeo's Values Orientation Survey based on original human values research of Prof Schwartz[103]

Scales	Description of people with high scores
Openness to change	
Self-direction – Thought	Likely to prefer being self-sufficient, enjoying working things out independently and forming own views
Self-direction – Action	Likely to prefer being free to make own decisions about life, what activities are undertaken and how these are planned
Stimulation	Likely to really enjoy new experiences, proactively looking for different things to do to make life more exciting
Hedonism	Likely to take advantage of every opportunity to have a good time, seeking to get as much pleasure out of life as possible

(Cont.)

Definitions of high scores for values used in Valpeo's Values Orientation Survey based on original human values research of Prof Schwartz[87] (cont.)

Scales	Description of people with high scores
	Self-enhancement
Achievement	Likely to be very ambitious and driven to succeed, taking delight in being recognised for achievements
Power – Dominance	Likely to really enjoy taking charge and having power, preferring to be in control and telling others what to do
Power – Resources	Likely to aspire to be wealthy and enjoy the power and control over resources that money can bring, taking pleasure in displaying wealth
Face	May have relatively little concern for having a good reputation, not caring much what others think
	Conservation
Personal security	Likely to be very concerned about avoiding risk, preferring not to take unnecessary, uncalculated or personal risks
Order and stability	Likely to be very keen for there to be order, stability and security, feeling very concerned when things are chaotic
Tradition and customs	Likely to be very eager to honour cultural, religious or family practices, maintaining traditional values and ways of thinking
Conformity to rules	Likely to want to obey all laws, rules and regulations, using rules to guide behaviour
Interpersonal conformity	Likely to be very keen to avoid upsetting or annoying other people, modifying actions and words accordingly

Scales	Description of people with high scores
Humility	Likely to feel that it is very important to be humble, being modest about own achievements
Self-transcendence	
Concern for nature	Likely to care deeply about nature, proactively and frequently taking part in activities to help protect the environment
Social justice and equality	Likely to care deeply about equal opportunities and ensuring that everyone is treated fairly, taking action to facilitate this
Tolerance	Likely to be tolerant towards all different kinds of people, appreciating the value in listening to the views of those who are different
Care	Likely to do everything possible to take care of loved ones, devoting considerable time and energy to showing concern and care for others
Dependability	Likely to be very keen to be considered completely dependable, reliable and trustworthy by everyone

Scales	Description of people with high scores
Humility	Likely to feel that it is very important to be humble, being modest about own achievements
Self-transcendence	
Concern for nature	Likely to care deeply about nature, proactively and frequently taking part in activities to help protect the environment
Social justice and equality	Likely to care deeply about equal opportunities and ensuring that everyone is treated fairly, taking action to facilitate this
Tolerance	Likely to be tolerant toward all different kinds of people, appreciating the value in listening to the views of those who are different
Care	Likely to do everything possible to take care of others, devoting considerable time and energy to showing concern and care for others
Dependability	Likely to be very keen to be considered completely dependable, reliable and trustworthy by everyone

Notes

1 World Economic Forum, *Future of Jobs Report 2023: Insight report* (2023), www3.weforum.org/docs/WEF_Future_of_Jobs_2023.pdf, accessed 22 August 2024

2 Manpower Group, '2024 Global talent shortage' (2024), https://go.manpowergroup.com/talent-shortage, accessed 22 August 2024

3 Mercer, *Global Talent Trends 2018 Study: Unlocking growth in the human age* (2018), https://info.mercer.com/rs/521-DEV-513/images/Talent-Trends-2018-Client-Deck-US_Canada%20FINAL.pdf, accessed 22 August 2024

4 K Coppé, 'Understanding drivers of commercial impact of technical experts using COSMOS and AIM', 2023. If you wish to access it, please contact Katarina via LinkedIn

5 SH Schwartz & J Cieciuch (2021). Measuring the Refined Theory of Individual Values in 49 Cultural Groups: Psychometrics of the Revised Portrait Value Questionnaire. Assessment 29, www.researchgate.net/publication/349058866, accessed 4 September 2024. The individual Values Orientation Survey used as part of this research is based on the original individual values work of Prof Schwartz and the questionnaire has recently been updated. Valpeo recently developed a new Behavioural

Orientation Survey in line with the European Federation of Psychologists' Associations standards and according to the best practice principles of the British Psychological Society (BPS): Both questionnaires are in the process of being accredited by the BPS. Valpeo, 'Valpeo dynamic tools' (2024), www.valpeo.com/valpeo-dynamics/valpeo-people-dynamics, accessed 22 August 2024. For the employee experience (EX) analysis, the EX questionnaire from Welliba (www.welliba.ai) was used.

6   N Tambe, 'Skills vs capabilities' (2023), www.neiltambe. com/blog/2013/07/23/skills-vs-capabilities, accessed 22 August 2024

7   World Economic Forum, *The Future of Jobs Report 2020* (2020), www.weforum.org/publications/the-future-of-jobs-report-2020, accessed 22 August 2024. The number of days is based on research conducted by Coursera, a skills learning provider. For more details please see the table on page 38 of the report.

8   'Conformity to rules' is one of the ten basic human values as developed by Prof Schwartz. SH Schwartz & J Cieciuch (2021). Measuring the Refined Theory of Individual Values in 49 Cultural Groups: Psychometrics of the Revised Portrait Value Questionnaire. Assessment 29, www.researchgate.net/ publication/349058866, accessed 4 September 2024

9   SH Schwartz & J Cieciuch (2021). Measuring the Refined Theory of Individual Values in 49 Cultural Groups: Psychometrics of the Revised Portrait Value Questionnaire. Assessment 29, www.researchgate.net/ publication/349058866, accessed 4 September 2024

10   Korn Ferry, 'Korn Ferry Institute study shows link between self-awareness and company financial performance' (2015), www.kornferry.com/about-us//press/korn-ferry-institute-study-shows-link-between-self-awareness-and-company-financial-performance, accessed 22 August 2024

11   T Eurich, 'What self-awareness really is (and how to cultivate it)', *Harvard Business Review* (2018), https://hbr. org/2018/01/what-self-awareness-really-is-and-how-to-cultivate-it, accessed 22 August 2024

12   Coppé K. Understanding drivers of commercial impact of technical experts using COSMOS and AIM - 2023

13   World Economic Forum, *Future of Jobs Report 2023: Insight report* (2023), www3.weforum.org/docs/WEF_Future_of_Jobs_2023.pdf, accessed 22 August 2024

14 Coppé K. Understanding drivers of commercial impact of technical experts using COSMOS and AIM - 2023

15 CEB Sales Executive Council Research, as cited in *The Challenger Sale*, 2011. © Challenger Performance Optimization, Inc

16 Challenger® and Mobilizer® are registered trademarks owned by Challenger Performance Optimization, Inc.

17 M Schultz, *Insight Selling* (Wiley, 2014)

18 CEB Sales Executive Council Research, as cited in *The Challenger Sale*, 2011. © Challenger Performance Optimization, Inc

19 J Barron, 'The ultimate guide to the B2B buyer's journey' (Cognism, 2023), www.cognism.com/blog/ultimate-guide-to-the-b2b-buyers-journey, accessed 22 August 2024

20 CEB Sales Executive Council Research, as cited in *The Challenger Sale*, 2015. © Challenger Performance Optimization, Inc

21 CEB Sales Executive Council Research, as cited in *The Challenger Sale*, 2011. © Challenger Performance Optimization, Inc

22 Gartner, *Win More B2B Sales Deals* (2018), www.gartner.com/en/sales/insights/win-more-b2b-sales-deals, accessed 22 August 2024 . This Gartner report is archived and is included for historical content only. GARTNER is a trademark of Gartner, Inc. and/or its affliates.

23 J Barron, 'The ultimate guide to the B2B buyer's journey' (Cognism, 2023), www.cognism.com/blog/ultimate-guide-to-the-b2b-buyers-journey, accessed 22 August 2024

24 M Dixon and T McKenna, *The Jolt Effect: How high performers overcome customer indecision* (Penguin Random House, 2022)

25 Gartner, *Why Accounts Aren't Growing, and What to Do About It* (2019), www.gartner.com/en/sales/trends/account-growth, accessed 22 August 2024 . This Gartner report is archived and is included for historical content only.

26 B Adamson, 'Driving Growth with Existing Customers' (2022), https://youtu.be/M5dAJ71RKJE?si=SssyVCC3IHiqi9QV, accessed 23 October 2024

27 CEB Sales Executive Council Research, as cited in *The Challenger Sale*, 2011. © Challenger Performance Optimization, Inc
The five typical profiles are lone wolf, Challenger, problem solver, relationship builder and hard worker.

28 De Tijd, 'Business travel dies out: "from six flights for a large contract to only three"' (2020), www.tijd.be/ondernemen/luchtvaart/de-zakenreis-sterft-uit-van-zes-vluchten-voor-groot-contract-naar-nog-slechts-drie/10247200.html, accessed 22 August 2024

29 CEB Sales Executive Council Research, as cited in *The Challenger Sale*, 2011. © Challenger Performance Optimization, Inc

30 Ibid

31 SR Levine and Thought Leaders, 'Diversity confirmed to boost innovation and financial results' (*Forbes*, 2020), www.forbes.com/sites/forbesinsights/2020/01/15/diversity-confirmed-to-boost-innovation-and-financial-results, accessed 22 August 2024

32 Gartner, 'What Sales Should Know About Modern B2B Buyers' (2019), www.gartner.com/smarterwithgartner/what-sales-should-know-about-modern-b2b-buyers. This Gartner content is archived and is included for historical context only.

33 I Montesdeoca, 'Six opportunities for demand and account-based marketing leaders in 2021' (Forrester, 2020), www.forrester.com/blogs/six-opportunities-for-demand-and-account-based-marketing-leaders-in-2021, accessed 22 August 2024

34 Mercer, *Global Talent Trends 2018 Study: Unlocking growth in the human age* (2018), https://info.mercer.com/rs/521-DEV-513/images/Talent-Trends-2018-Client-Deck-US_Canada%20FINAL.pdf, accessed 22 August 2024

35 Gartner, 'CSO Update: The new B2B buying journey and its implication for sales' (2019), www.gartner.com.au/en/sales/insights/b2b-buying-journey, accessed 22 August 2024 . This Gartner content is archived and is included for historical context only.

36 Gartner, 'Why Accounts Aren't Growing, and What to Do About It' (2019), www.gartner.com/en/sales/trends/account-growth, accessed 5 September 2024

37 CEB Sales Executive Council Research, as cited in *The Challenger Sale*, 2011. © Challenger Performance Optimization, Inc

38 World Economic Forum in collaboration with Willis Towers Watson, 'Human Capital as an Asset: An accounting framework to reset the value of talent in the new world

of work' (2020), www3.weforum.org/docs/WEF_NES_
HR4.0_Accounting_2020.pdf, accessed 22 August 2024

39 Gartner, 'Three lessons to sustain workforce resilience
through disruption' (2021), www.gartner.com/
smarterwithgartner/3-lessons-to-sustain-workforce-
resilience-through-disruption, accessed 22 August 2024.
This Gartner content is archived and is included for
historical context only.

40 Gartner, 'Make way for a more human-centric
employee value proposition' (2021), www.gartner.com/
smarterwithgartner/make-way-for-a-more-human-centric-
employee-value-proposition, accessed 22 August 2024. This
Gartner content is archived and is included for historical
context only.

41 M Dixon and T McKenna, *The Jolt Effect: How high
performers overcome customer indecision* (Penguin Random
House, 2022)

42 Wharton Executive Education, 'The Enterprise Mindset:
An Integrated Business Approach' (July 2021), https://
executiveeducation.wharton.upenn.edu/thought-
leadership/wharton-at-work/2021/07/the-enterprise-
mindset-integrated-approach, accessed 5 September 2024

43 CEB Sales Executive Council Research, as cited in *The
Challenger Customer*, 2015. © Challenger Performance
Optimization, Inc.

44 Ibid

45 Ibid

46 Ibid

47 Ibid

48 Ibid

49 M Dixon and T McKenna, *The Jolt Effect: How high
performers overcome customer indecision* (Penguin Random
House, 2022)

50 ibid

51 CEB Sales Executive Council Research, as cited in
The Challenger Sale, 2011. © Challenger Performance
Optimization, Inc.

52 Gartner, *CSO Update: The new B2B buying journey and
its implication for sales* (2019), www.gartner.com.au/en/
sales/insights/b2b-buying-journey, accessed 22 August
2024. This Gartner content is archived and is included for
historical context only.

53 CEB Sales Executive Council Research, as cited in
    The Challenger Sale, 2011. © Challenger Performance
    Optimization, Inc.
54 CEB Sales Executive Council Research, as cited in
    The Challenger Sale, 2015. © Challenger Performance
    Optimization, Inc.
55 M Dixon and T McKenna, *The Jolt Effect: How high
    performers overcome customer indecision* (Penguin Random
    House, 2022)
56 R Noyes, 'How to cultivate cross-silo leadership' (INSEAD
    Knowledge, 2019), https://knowledge.insead.edu/
    leadership-organisations/how-cultivate-cross-silo-
    leadership, accessed 22 August 2024
57 K Kelly, *The Inevitable: Understanding the 12 technological
    forces that will shape our future* (Penguin, 2017)
58 F Gino, 'The business case for curiosity: research
    shows that it leads to higher-performing, more-adaptable
    firms', *Harvard Business Review* (2018), https://hbr.
    org/2018/09/the-business-case-for-curiosity, accessed
    22 August 2024
59 S Jang, 'Cultural brokerage and creative performance in
    multicultural teams', *Organization Science*, 28/6 (2017), 993–
    1009, https://doi.org/10.1287/orsc.2017.1162
60 CEB Sales Executive Council Research, as cited in
    The Challenger Sale, 2015. © Challenger Performance
    Optimization, Inc.
61 H Hoeken and D O'Keefe, 'Message design choices
    don't make much difference to persuasiveness and
    can't be counted on—not even when moderating
    conditions are specified', *Frontiers in Psychology*
    (2021), www.frontiersin.org/journals/psychology/
    articles/10.3389/fpsyg.2021.664160/full, accessed
    22 August 2024
62 M Dixon and T McKenna, *The Jolt Effect: How high
    performers overcome customer indecision* (Penguin Random
    House, 2022)
63 Ibid
64 CEB Sales Executive Council Research, as cited in The
    Challenger Customer, 2011. © Challenger Performance
    Optimization, Inc.
65 Challenger, www.challengerinc.com

66 M Dixon and T McKenna, *The Jolt Effect: How high performers overcome customer indecision* (Penguin Random House, 2022

67 Ibid

68 R Bolton and D Bolton, *Social Style / Management Style: Developing productive work relationships* (Amacom, 1984), *People Styles at Work*, New York, American Management Association, 1996; HR Leadership Academy research

69 T Casciaro, AC Edmondson and S Jang, 'Cross-silo leadership: how to create more value by connecting experts from inside and outside the organization', *Harvard Business Review* (2019), www.hbs.edu/faculty/Pages/item.aspx?num=56041, accessed 22 August 2024

70 CEB Sales Executive Council Research, as cited in *The Challenger Customer*, 2015. © Challenger Performance Optimization, Inc.

71 Ibid

72 Gartner, 'Reshaping leadership to prepare for the future' (2019), www.gartner.com/en/documents/3947464, accessed 22 August 2024. This Gartner content is archived and is included for historical context only.

73 We are Unity in partnership with Macquarie University, *COVID-19: Crisis or Catalyst?* (2020), https://research-management.mq.edu.au/ws/portalfiles/portal/125535985/MQ_WAU_COVID_REPORT_2020.pdf, accessed 22 August 2024

74 Gartner, 'Reshaping leadership to prepare for the future' (2019), www.gartner.com/en/documents/3947464, accessed 22 August 2024. This Gartner content is archived and is included for historical context only.

75 Enterprise Leadership Survey analysis, CEB 2014

76 Accenture, 'The Future of Work' (2022), www.accenture.com/us-en/insights/consulting/future-work, accessed 5 September 2024

77 D Ulrich, 'How to increase the impact of your talent initiatives' (LinkedIn, 2020), www.linkedin.com/pulse/how-increase-impact-your-talent-initiatives-dave-ulrich, accessed 22 August 2024

78 E Pulakos and R Kaiser, 'Don't let teamwork get in the way of agility', *Harvard Business Review* (2020), https://hbr.org/2020/05/dont-let-teamwork-get-in-the-way-of-agility, accessed 22 August 2024

79 Forrester Consulting, *Employee Performance Management Needs Promotion: How to transform the performance process from an annual chore to a continuous value driver* (HRreview, 2018), https://hrreview.co.uk/white-papers/employee-performance-management/115175, accessed 22 August 2024

80 K Coppé, 'Understanding drivers of commercial impact of technical experts using COSMOS and AIM', 2023

81 Gartner (formerly CEB), 'Six Ways to Fix Performance Management', CEB 2012 High Performing Survey (n= 23,339) and CEB 2014 Enterprise Contribution Workforce survey (n=10,531). This Gartner content is archived and is included for historical context.

82 ibid

83 T Chamorro-Premuzic, *Personality and Individual Differences*, 3rd Edition (Wiley, 2015)

84 Valpeo, Behavioural Orientation Survey, 'Valpeo dynamic tools' (2024), www.valpeo.com/valpeo-dynamics/valpeo-people-dynamics, accessed 22 August 2024

85 Ibid

86 **Correlation is significant at the 0.01 level (2-tailed) and personality traits have coefficients of >.35.

87 Ibid

88 SH Schwartz & J Cieciuch (2021). Measuring the Refined Theory of Individual Values in 49 Cultural Groups: Psychometrics of the Revised Portrait Value Questionnaire. Assessment 29, www.researchgate.net/publication/349058866, accessed 4 September 2024

89 The Schwartz Value Orientation Survey; visual and updated assessment created by Valpeo

90 **Correlation is significant at the 0.01 level (2-tailed) and personality traits have coefficients of >.30 apart from Independent Thought which has a coefficient of 0.293°°.

91 T Casciaro, AC Edmondson and S Jang, 'Cross-silo leadership: how to create more value by connecting experts from inside and outside the organization', *Harvard Business Review* (2019)

92 K Coppé, 'Understanding drivers of commercial impact of technical experts using COSMOS and AIM', 2023

93 B Morgan, 'The state of customer experience study 2017' (*Forbes*, 2017), www.forbes.com/sites/blakemorgan/2017/10/31/the-state-of-customer-

experience-study-2017/?sh=48b819a12ae4, accessed 22 August 2024

94 Forrester Consulting, 'Close the employee experience gap', A Forrester Consulting thought leadership paper commissioned by SAP SuccessFactors, Qualtrics and Ernst & Young LLP (2021), https://www.documentonews.gr/wp-content/uploads/2021/03/603f1f0a825e636aa57d7cd2.pdf, accessed 11 March 2025

95 Welliba, *Definition of Employee Experience: What it is, what it is not, and why you should care* (2022), www.welliba.com/science, accessed 5 September 2024

96 Welliba is a provider of an Employee Experience Management System based on the best of behavioural science and human-centric technology to improve people and business outcomes for individuals, teams and organisations: www.welliba.com.

97 Correlation is significant at the 0.05 level (2-tailed) and EX dimensions linked to outcome statements from participants have coefficients of >.35.

98 Welliba, *The Power of Employee Experience: Predicting business metrics with the Welliba EX Index* (2023)

99 Ibid

100 Willis Towers Watson, 'Infographic: employee experience a top priority for 9 in 10 employers around the globe' (2021), www.wtwco.com/en-us/insights/2021/06/employee-experience-a-top-priority-for-9-in-10-employers-around-the-globe, accessed 22 August 2024

101 Accenture, *Care to Do Better* (2020), www.accenture.com/content/dam/accenture/final/a-com-migration/thought-leadership-assets/accenture-care-to-do-better-report.pdf, accessed 22 August 2024

102 Valpeo, 'Valpeo dynamic tools' (2024), www.valpeo.com/valpeo-dynamics/valpeo-people-dynamics, accessed 22 August 2024

103 Ibid

104 J Brazier, 'Exclusive: Welliba crowned winner of the UNLEASH Startup 2024 Award!' (2024), www.unleash.ai/unleash-world/exclusive-welliba-crowned-winner-of-the-unleash-startup-2024-award, accessed 23 October 2024

Acknowledgements

I never thought that I would write a book, but now that I have, I'll admit I got more than a little help along the way. My father was the first person who made me think about commercial impact – when I was a child, he taught me how to convince people to buy postcards and gadgets for charitable organisations. I quickly understood that different messages appealed to different people. He would have loved to know that this book exists, but unfortunately, he passed away before it was completed. I am grateful that both my parents always stimulated me to pursue new ideas.

At CEB, Anthony Parslow allowed our commercial enablement team to test many tools, concepts and best practices in a global organisation, many of which I have incorporated in this book.

Louisa Tate ran all the psychometric analyses for the preferred Values and Behaviours of technical experts. Fabiaan Van Vrekhem let me use his new psychometric tools for my international study. Shanthi Senathirajah and Sera Goktas helped me with the international research analysis and proofreading. Jan Lewis made sure my manuscript and graphics looked good before submission to Rethink Press. The Rethink Press team (especially Tess, Anke and Eve) came up with many useful suggestions.

Emmy Hackett and Rowena Cooper were great sound-boards. David Barrett and the founders of Welliba agreed to let Welliba's Science Team (Maximilian Jansen and Richard Justenhoven) review how my models were related to the concept of employee experience. Matt Dixon, Brent Adamson and Ted McKenna wrote inspiring books (*The Challenger Sale*, *The Challenger Customer* and *The Jolt Effect*) that were influential for my development.

There are of course many friends and (ex) colleagues who have been a great soundboard along the way.

I hope this book will inspire my two kids, Anna and Lucas, to step out of their comfort zones, grab every opportunity to learn, persist, and to finish what they start.

Last but certainly not least, I want to thank Rob, my partner, whose patience was essential. Not only because he reviewed the manuscript more times than he cares to remember, but because he also took over a lot of the work for our kids and the home we made for them, so that I could spend more time researching and writing. I am grateful.

The Author

In the twenty-four years of her professional career, Katarina Coppé worked in sales, HR consulting, commercial enablement, and learning and development across many different countries. While working for CEB and Gartner, she was privileged to be able to access the latest best-in-class research in sales and HR and in a position to apply and experiment with these best practices in many different audiences of a global and complex B2B organisation. After many years designing and implementing behavioural change and skills programmes for sales and delivery teams, Katarina set up a learning and development function which targeted a broader audience, leading change for all leaders, managers and individual contributors on programmes such as performance management, onboarding and manager development. In her last role as head of learning and development, she witnessed how silos in organisations can leave strategic change programmes losing traction until they get stranded.

The most impactful experience which helped Katarina see the importance of structural alignment of sales, presales, delivery and other technical experts was the roll-out of the Challenger sales methodology. This approach has been proven to deliver results through many years of practical evidence and numerous studies. She has seen many situations in which commercial potential was available and unlocked by the correct application of customer improvement behaviours and coaching. The outcomes were clearly visible: growth in revenue, client loyalty and business growth.

On average, one sales framework or methodology was launched every four years in the organisation where Katarina worked. The choice of a new functional model or framework was always driven by the C-suite executive in seat at the time, but driving change, especially in a global organisation, is hard if it is not embedded in the organisation or second nature to all stakeholders involved in the end-to-end sales and client delivery process. All stakeholders need to have some central oversight.

For over six years, Katarina worked in a central commercial enablement team to create oversight across key tools, processes (including delivery of solutions), content, development support, frameworks and digital resources. As part of the team, she translated the commercial strategy into needs and wants for different teams to help them innovate and execute. The role of the technical expert in this process and the impact they can have was clear to her. Many organisations forget to map out the role and impact of the technical experts as part of this end-to-end customer journey and lose sight of offering them tailored support to provide purpose and commercial development.

Why does she focus on technical experts? Katarina sees herself as a technical expert, one in the domain of HR, specialised in predicting and developing behaviours and experiences at work. She became fascinated in the link between HR and sales best practices in B2B and how better alignment between these proven sciences can drive commercial impact and develop commercial behaviours in sales and non-sales audiences.

After using her inhouse expertise in a global learning and development role, and some time as a go-to-market advisor to human capital organisations, she now works with like-minded individuals in Welliba who are on a mission to disrupt traditional employee engagement, EX, listening and development approaches. Welliba applies behavioural science, AI and EX management technology to help organisations benchmark themselves effectively and access personalised insight and guidance at scale to help employees, managers and organisations simultaneously reach better outcomes. In October 2024, Welliba won Unleash World's prestigious Startup Award 2024, voted by an international jury of industry experts.[104]

You can contact Katarina at:

🌐 www.customerimprovementselling.com

in www.linkedin.com/in/katarina-coppé-734455

9 781781 338940